DEADLY LEY LINES

DEADLY LEY LINES
Healing World Trauma

Composed and Composited
by
Peter Champoux

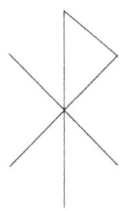

First published in the USA

© Peter Champoux 2024
Peter Champoux: Author, Typeset and Book Design

All rights reserved.

Any part of this book may be reproduced or transmitted in any form or by any means, with attribution.

For information, address:
peter.champoux@gmail.com

Public Domain image rights retained by creator and curator.
Map use granted by: Mile High Maps, Google Earth.

Cover Design, Text, collage and illustrations: Peter Champoux

Type font, Verdana, Microsoft Corporation.
Adobe CS 2024: InDesign, Illustrator, Photoshop, Acrobat
Print and Distribution service: ImgramSpark
Cover Image: Lagoon Nebula; NASA-Hubble Telescope

Titles by Peter Champoux; *Gaia Matrix, Ark of Antero, and Moon Rivers,* available on www.geometryofplace.com and www.purespiritwaters.org

freedom

Contents

PREFACE...**11**

INTRODUCTION.......................................**13**

SILK ROAD LEY.......................................**19**

GREAT PYRAMID....................................**26**

On the Road to Mecca................27

North by North West..................28

Latitude with Attitude................32

NORTH to KYIV..........................33

X Marks the Spot........................36

South by West............................41

42°NORTH LATITUDE...............................**44**

First Nations Ley.......................................**60**

OUR WOUNDED KNEE..................66

PATRIARCHY in POLARITY.......................**80**

Acadia Ley 80

Arcadia Ley 85

Beijing Ley..**89**

Crossing Waves..98

Great Pyramid 99

Boston, Massachusetts 99

Three Borders 100

Fertile Crescent 101

Rogue Waves 101

Answering the Call 102

CONCLUSION...103

PREFACE

This, the fourth in a series of books, arose from observations made over five decades of living, thinking and breathing the cultural use of stone. Not an academic or author, this book offers some observations and anecdotes gathered over those decades on the nature of what is popularly known as 'ley lines'.

A nonfiction work, it was composed without footnote for validation of its theory, as no academic would venture to research invisible lines whose proof is correlative. Composited for those with a "spectrum" in mind, like my dyslexic self, ADHD friendly font and graphic rendition of accompanying text was used to make this book accessible to all. If the reader finds a subject or statement of interest, Grandfather Google will answer all your queries.

Earning a living in construction, my primary trade was that of a stone mason. If I can cite any source for this knowledge base, I am compelled to communicate to the world, it arose from this transformation of rock into stone. In anthroposophic lectures by Rudolf Steiner he observed that whenever a rock is split into stone a Gnome of Knowledge is released. It is far-fetched I know, but it is my belief that Earth itself, over these decades, taught me about itself which I impart to you the reader. Feeling about in the dark, these books are attempts to frame an emerging new art and science of a living Earth, Gaiagraphy.

My funny jewish-french name, with both pe and poux in its sounding, gave direction to look towards its translation 'rock of the field', at the start of this life long effort to scribe this new world view

More than the material statistics of geography, the Earth is a spiritual being, an earth-cell with a membrane consciousness or 'field'. Maintaining the integrity of the Earth's fields: physical, spiritual, astral, and etheric—

are essential to the work of quantum geo-stathis for 5th dimensional stewards of the Earth. Providing a subjective overview of Earth's leys lines, it is hoped this book objectifies our spaceship Earth traveling the cosmos.

Cultural corridors and pathways of history, 'Deadly Ley Lines' is sadly the history of war. A struggle endemic to free-will, the trauma triangles described herein are R-Rated human struggles.

A long time student of comparative religion and short term student of anthroposophy I use spiritual terms I enjoy. Please do not mistake this as promoting a particular religious philosophy, encouraging the reader to instead translate these terms to those appropriate to themselves.

Published at a time when a collective consciousness comes into relationship, via instantaneous world wide web awareness of world events, an empathic response to the 'other' is cultivated. Objectifying the manipulation of the despots of the world promotes a sovereign-self expression of the One Source-One Force. Further, confronted with an ever changing biosphere, this book shows how human emotion affects the world. Healthful operation of spaceship earth's systems is a prerequisite to traveling the stars with our galactic community. It is offered in the pages of this book a knowledge base useful to this future.

as holy blood worldwide from its heights. At the threshold of Temple Mount's Wailing Wall, the world asks forgiveness for the destruction of the 2nd Temple by Rome's Titus; whose spirit still beats down those who would revolt against: Pharaoh, Caesar, King, and Sultan.

Even Jesus got in on the action in his attempt to redeem the effects of this curse in his building of an etheric temple of love for all the Earth with Christ in the etheric. Watered by the blood and spit this city of peace is of little refuge for those who would live in brotherly love.

After an ever so brief visit to Israel we reach our ley's lowest point in the 'Dead Sea' borderlands with Jordan. At the bottom of the Jordan Rift Valley it 1000 foot depth and 1,412 feet below sea level this lake is a pool of memory preserved in salt. Thought to be the location of Sodom and Gomorrah, the tale of these two cities as an epitome of sin, its destruction by fire and sulfur is watched over by the silent salty remains of Lot's wife Sarah.

In Roman times Amman, Jordan was called Philadelphia, the city of brotherly love. At the crossroads with another man is tied up in the Gordian Knot that is the Holy Land. Once an annex of Jordan the West Bank was fought over, again, alongside Egypt in a Six Day War against Israel, and lost. Jordan is now the unheard peacemaker in this din of Djinn. Sweeping over the river Jordan in a wave of sacrificial blood, Jordan's rock is stained red as it rolls into ancient Babylon.

A question arises, who laid down this road of blood and oil and sand and rock across this ancient historic expanse? Penned into existence, the zionist state of Israel was made, when the world was distracted by WWII, through the efforts of a one Lord Ba(a)lfour of England, suggesting through adagram this agreement was 'for baal'.

Creeping like a thief in the night the spirit of Ahriman profits from the suffering of this world of sorrows. Like the black oil that flows just below desert sand Ahriman's deadly ley line enters the 'Fertile Crescent' of the Tigris-Euphrates river cultures of Babylon and Baghdad.

Saddam Hussein despot tyranny, Baghdad was burned under the Bush presidencies. Nearby holy city to Shia Muslims, Karabala, marks the divide in Islam, western Sunni versus eastern Shia. Since Cain and Abel had their epic brawl, corpus have piled as roadbed across the Fertile Crescent as appeasement, this to Sumerian swamp god Enki.

A once great city Baghdad is now laid to ruin by successive invasions from east, west and from within by those whose misuse of will for power's sake turned garden paradise into waste.

INTRODUCTION

Deadly ley lines! Who would think? Or, then again, what is a ley line? Ley lines in popular copy tend to attribute qualities of the good ole days when human culture was more attuned to the rhythms of nature. Rainbows and unicorns, that type of thing. There has been a great interest in recent years in ley lines, brought to the fore by programming on the History Channel and such. British Society of Dowsers posits in their 'Dragon Project' that leys only exist in England where five or more megalithic sites are found in alignment over a length of five miles.

When imagining the world grid of ley lines, the go-to models are the Plutonic geometrics of regular solids (tetrahedron, cube, octahedron, icosahedron, dodecahedron) projected as ley lines keyed to Earth's poles and Great Pyramid. While nice and neat this model bears little resemblance to ley patterns of geographic and cultural alignments typically found with leys of old. Leys are a mystery whose existence in collective imagination is real. Leys are like the wind and water (Feng Shui), they are a transparent substance seen in their effect on nature and culture. An elemental substance best attributed to ether. Yes, invisible lines in so many words.

Stepping back before going further ahead, leys were first coined by a 19th-century antiquarian named Alfred Watkins. Alfred noticed in his travels as a salesman-researcher that place and family names associated with ley lines, or as he preferred 'straight tracks', had been named with the suffix 'ley' attached, suggesting them to be ley keepers as it was the form of the day to take the name of one's occupation. John Michell in his 'View over Atlantis' furthered Watkins' work and ushered in and popularized 'ley hunting" in the 20th and 21st centuries.

Ley lines have been given human attributes as an anthropomorphized planetary nervous and acupuncture system. Indeed standing stones have been called lithopuncture needles. The leys of old England and mainland Europe and their attendant mounds, stone circles, and dolmens must have had a purpose and been a utility of value to warrant such a prodigious effort to construct. It would also seem that this system failed to function at some point and was abandoned.

A world-wide megalithic system, its ruin is seen in pyramids and calendar sites suggesting a planetary environmental collapse that weakened earth's fields enough to make this approach to agriculture no longer viable.

To what degree this collapse affected this earth-energy system can never be fully known. It is evident from history that those cultures that participated benefited and benefit to this day. A question arises, as to how much this megalith foundation had on England's success worldwide. The time keeping of Stonehedge certainly heralds England's dominion over the 4th dimension of time on its Prime Meridian.

The grass is sweeter, according to the cows, along megalithic cultural corridors. Bone record in archeology attests to better health associated with megalithic implementation. Those with "vision" saw the megaliths glow with a kind of blue plasma, and crop circles have been seen to be laid down by orbs of plasma near these ancient sites. One might imagine an ancient world when its atmosphere was more charged by a more coherent magnetic field than today—a field whose charge was grounded through this system to propagate extreme crop growth with its infusion of sky nitrogen and geomagnetism. When Earth's field weakened to near collapse, as it is today, so did this method of agriculture.

Aligned to the sunrise at Beltane (May 3), England's Grand Ley and French Brittany's Carnac stones both orient southwest to the Azore Islands on the Mid Atlantic Rift. Located on this mid-Atlantic expansion fault zone the Azores were cited as the location of Atlantis in Plato's Timaeus, "southwest of the Gates of Hercules (Rock of Gibraltar)"; suggesting megaliths may have been a part of the telluric system of power the Atlantians mastered.

Excavating some of the ancient mounds in the south of England, buried in these mounds, dolmans (made of three upright stones capped with a single stone slab) were found to have a melted surface. A kind of battery, these mounds comprised layers of magnetic and paramagnetic soils. Given the 5000 degrees necessary to melt rock, lightning must have played a part in this agricultural system with repeated strikes of sky nitrogen.

Expanding upon this view over Atlantis we can see leys as a conduit for piezoelectric circuits; directing plasma collected by standing stone, stored in a mound, and transmitted into the field via stone circles with appropriate timing. Many if not all stone circles associated with the megalithic systems were tuned to take advantage of the 18.6 year lunar max cycle when the Moon's plasma discharge was at its greatest.

While the British Society of Dowser insists leys only exist in England a similar natural phenomenon has been attributed by other cultures: Australian "black fellas" as "song lines" emerging from "dreamtime", the South American indigenous "spirit lines", and by Asian peoples as "dragon lines". This universality of experience suggest something may be up here and it is not specific to just England. There have been many fine accounts written about these systems under the moniker of geomancy (earth magic) and geodesy (earth measure), and as this author prefers, gaiagraphy (patterns of the living earth).

In the Gaia Hypothesis by Lovelock/Margulis:1972, it was concluded that the Earth was alive and self-regulating similar to a single-cell organism. A treatise on gas regulation in Earth's atmosphere it brought to collective consciousness an impulse towards self-regulation based on organic methods for environmental sustainability. Given that "IT'S ALIVE '' what biological contribution do these integral worldwide ley-song-spirit-dragon lines have to Earth-cell regulatory systems?

Pathways for weather, angels and demons, culture, and war; these leys are lines of consciousness. Engaging with earth-cell through its ley system shifts human/terran life from a parasitic to a co-creative biostasis.

Before the demonizing of the Earth by church and state, making its exploitation and environmental destruction a mandate, spiritual acts of world maintenance were enacted along Earth's meridian systems in the cyclic manner ordained by the movements laid down in 'star knowledge', benefiting life.

Research by Rory Duff of England has chronicled, via dowsing, that dual pole ley lines change into coherent waveforms when Earth passes through solar plasma sheets every eighth day. Fractal in scale glactic plasma sheet has its effect every 25,000 years, harmonizing the Earth about now.

Recent astrophysical models show another such plasma wave undulating through the Milky Way's galactic plane. A 'ghost in the machine' of stellar mechanics, the procession of the equinoxes every 25,000 years, renews Earth's magnetic field with a magnetic pole reversal, like the pole reversal occurring today. When a dynmo changes spin direction what happens to the magnetic poles?

Intuitives such as Dr. Rudolf Steiner have shown how human emotions affect the weather. Also well known, are the effects of lunacy when the full moon discharges solar plasma as feedback into and through Earth's ley system, as we pass through Earth's electromagnetic tail. It is well known by medical personnel that plasma periods are when menses flow, more births and deaths occur, and mental disorders blossom as brain storms—as human and oceanic tides rise to the moon's pull.

Geologic record from the bandwidths of new rock being laid down on the mid-Atlantic rift shows a magnetic pole reversal every 20,000 or so years. This periodic pole shift generates a strengthening of Earth's magnetic field. Occuring when a weakened mixed polarity field is followed by a coherent equatorial demarcation of north and south polarity. With the Earth on the cusp of this 20,000-year galactic pulse, stellar photonic plasma is increasing leading to warming planets. The change in sunlight from orange to white, and an entropic magnetic field indicates we are in for a ride. Electro-mechanics has it that when polarity is reversed in a dynamo its direction of spin also changes. Evidence of this Earth spin reversal is found in the Andes Mountains, where geologists observed the Andes appear to have been thrown up in a day. Such a spin reversal would result in lithosphere adjustment in this scale.

When rock is put under pressure, even from something as slight as a hammer blow, there is an increase in the piezoelectric charge of rock. A worldwide hammer blow would, in effect, renew earth's life-preserving field. So empowered, a ley system of earth energies would come online once again. As an added benefit, surfing these galaxy plasma waves upgrades in DNA are seen in the archaeological record from Neanderthal to Cro-magnon to Homo Sapien to...Homo Spiritus. Learning to manage such civilization-ending reversals is necessary to advance without going through this wash-and-repeat cycle. It is imagined that through Earth maintenance, such changes can be minimized by understanding and utilizing Earth's ley systems.

As we enter into a renewal phase of the Earth, its ley lines are at their lowest degenerate energetic state. Turning an eye towards the renewal process of Earth energies to come, preparation must be made. As the Earth was stripped of its telluric vitality, by solar radiation and galactic zones of dissonance, frequencies of discord penetrated Earth and solar system as it moved through a galactic plasma trough filled with a negative polarity. Earth's ley system focused and transmitted this dissonance throughout the planet's body. Preparing this ley system to release these old frequencies we take in new incoming light codes, awakening Earth and humanity.

Varied as a phenomena, ley lines represent a relationship with the etheric Earth. One finds a ley here through dowsing and there through patterns of culture and nature. The methods used in this treaty exclude dowsing in favor of a pattern language of earth energies seen in the alignments of geography. Given leys are seen as part of the living earth, perhaps 'gaiagraphy' patterns are more to the point. While many have their take on ley lines, I can only speak to my own.

In a way, it is a sovereign relationship with the spiritual world and Creator. Because ley lines are not mentioned in most religious texts, adherents think them unimportant because of their exclusion by those in full knowledge. Like a radio frequency, it all depends on the tuning as to whether hip-hop or the classics are played. The fact that there are so many differing experiences surrounding ley lines is proof of their existence as only something of substance would solicit a broad spectrum of appreciation.

The proof of the historic Jesus' conquering death is found in the effects of the etheric Christ on sovereign souls. Experiencing God's love through Christ in the etheric Earth is his proof experienced in the human heart. Not on the same level as Christ consciousness, ley lines are more in the realm of the Elementals who also are in-service-to-others in supersensible realities. The evil attributed to the earth by religions comes down to the use of free will. Christ changed all that when he implored "...thy will be done, on (in) the Earth as it is in Heaven". It is taking a while to fully permeate, but Christ in the etheric continues, purging willful evil through the ley systems of Earth.

The residue of this evil continues to flow through leys as a nervous system addicted to a bad habit. Whose will is to be done? The vices? Hitler's? The Khans? Discorporated Corporations? Ahriman? For all of those who are at play in the impressionable programmable deadly ley lines, the etheric Christ clears the deadly ley lines through willful sacrifice to humanity.

The Templar's system of Gothic cathedrals was constructed on ley lines to support the great work of Christ consciousness in Europe and the planet. Birthed through their Marian cathedral technology, Christ presence, as a syncretic overlay, infused Christ into the ley lines through a syncretism of pagan sacred landscape.

Faith works as a mutually supportive field of consciousness. Agreeing upon a spiritual reality that recognizes the presence of an evil counterforce, push back occurs through shared prayers and intentions. Demon slayers who have made it their work to remove such malevolence are kept real busy, as all discordant energies have the impulse to return to Love and the good.

While many other leys are identifiable, the ones needing clearing are identified here. Like an old bad habit, the leys identified here, through faith-filled awareness, can shift these deadly ley lines from service-to-self to service-to-others.

It was observed that if one drew on a map all the various etheric earth energy lines on a paper map with a pencil it would cover the map in graphite. There are creation forces everywhere. In groups questions arise, "where are the ley lines in this or that country?" or "are there ley lines through my house?" A phenomena in scale, they exist in the etheric as signals detectable by their effect, intuition, and a connection with nature's spirit. In pristine wilderness, such leys are typically healthy. Where war and blood has been shed in hatred, leys retreat or suffer under the yoke of traumatic emotions. Highways, quarry operations, clear-cuts, war zones, electro-smog, and urban blight all suppress vitality and often result in geopathic zones. It is to these geopathic lines that attention is focused and a call made for their healing. Entrained with the habit of war, exposing their dissonance is a first step towards recovery in the knowledge that deadly ley lines exist.

The allegorical story about the blind men and the elephant applies to ley research. Like God and elephants, ley lines are larger than life and subject to interpretation by each individual 'ley hunter', earth energy researcher, or religion. All of them think only they know the true nature of the elephant. It's a great tree, it's a great wind, it's a great snake, it's a great trumpet, etc.... The elephant in this perspective sees ley lines as a cultural corridor whose passage is determined by an alignment of historic events, cities, and nature. This emotion of war has been a part of the human experience over the last galactic cycle. This condition may be difficult to read about, as much as it is to write about, as it exposes the dark habits of war entrained like an inflamed sciatic nerve whose 'Groundhog's Day' is destined to repeat until humanity (and Bill Murry) gets it right by being in service-to-others.

Deadly ley lines are the result of the misuse of free-will by young souls learning to wield will's power in earth-school. Reincarnating into this planet of sorrows for lifetimes is a crucible for soul's refinement and willful alignment of humanity 'Toward the One'. Transforming these deadly leys to lively leys is accomplished through the use of free-will. Directed as free-willed intention into its 'field', you the reader can change its deadly frequency and change the manifestation of its mass with the use of will as a power for good in the world.

SILK ROAD LEY

The first in our exploration of 'deadly ley lines' is called the Silk Road Ley as it connects the Middle East and the Mediterranean Sea with the Pacific Ocean's Hong Kong in a 5,018-mile (8,075km) arc of conflict. Feeling this crease in our elephant's hide we move from west to east starting in the fertile fan of the Nile Delta. This great fan of water vitality has a geometric nexus on the Great Pyramid that we will see in later chapters as the radiating source of many such conflicted ley lines.

As a preview it is along this ley we find the cursed Gaza Strip, blessed Jerusalem, Amman, fertile crescent of Baghdad, Iran, Kabul, Islamabad, the border conflicts at the west and east ends of the Himalayas, Lhasa, and schizophrenic Hong Kong.

In this era alone war has been marching across this ley in a consecutive series of conflicts. With Western powers pushing east and Eastern powers pushing westward with explosive force devastation laid waste to lands and peoples with depleted uranium shelling. Then there were the Mongol Hordes, and conquering Constantine, both of whom brought destruction without contribution beyond service-to-self. USSR, USA, NATO, and now the Taliban have tried, as Constantine did, to break the spirit and sovereignty of Kabul's Afghanistan to no avail beyond suffering. Leaving a legacy of retreating life waters from the fires of war in a deadly triangle of trauma's emotion.

The British empire's dividing of Ottoman countries along nontraditional bio-regional boundaries ensured continuing conflict between peoples and future geopolitical instability. One may conclude it to be patriarchy at its dysfunctional finest. What is evil other than the misuse of one's free will over another?

Springing from the pyramidal top-down economics and Nile River bulrushes that gave Moses a second chance at life, this Silk Road deadly ley line crosses the Suez Canal's grand accomplishment only to make landfall in the Gaza Strip's near the once great Canaanite city of Ashkelon.

Cursed by the Pharaoh's priest, the spring-fed Canaanite city of Ashkelon was an impregnable fortress of heretics living outside the balance of Egyptian goddess Maat in their monotheistic, human sacrifice,worship of the rain god Baal. This curse, described on the Merneptah Stele, set the frequency for this ley and all Canaanite lands that make up present-day Israel/Palestine.

Seemingly this curse favors the invading force. The Egyptians were at a loss to stop this breakaway colony as impregnable Ashkelon had spring water, high walls, access to the sea, and an endless supply of pigs. The pigs would eat the dead and the living would eat the pigs, giving cause for Jewish, and some Christian prohibition of pork as a cannibalism one set removed..

This curse against Canaan was written on clay bowls, filled with water to give this curse life, and broken to ensure it never could be undone. This curse intoned that whoever revolted or spoke of revolt would be destroyed by their actions, across lands of Cannaan. Whether or not you believe in curses, the history of these lands has had one successive "crusade" after another, with European Jews being the latest crusade in its centuries-old bloodletting to appease Baal's blood lust.

As a punctuation mark on this curse, I completed this account in early December 2023 when Hamas revolted and Israel responded with a slaughter of the innocent as yet another offering to Baal.

In effect this curse is directed at monotheism. Without a need of a curse to have such effects, monotheism has served as an adversary to the One Force-One Force, who would keep the Human spirit in check and under fear's control. In Man's state of amnesia, to imagine the will of the Divine is a blasphemy to others who attest to knowing a differing truth, lead to the endless religious wars of the "holy land".

A deadly 200 miles along this blood soaked Silk Road Ley we set foot in the holy city of Jerusalem. Beloved Jerusalem was cut in two, ignoring the wisdom of Solomon into East and West Jerusalem now whose two mothers mourn the blood of their innocent.

A place worth bleeding for Jerusalem is underlain by the closest thing to living rock, limestone. A kind of planetary neruo-ganglia, Jerusalem limestone transmits Golgotha's Christ Mystery

After failing to find the weapons of mass destruction, wielded by its merchants of war, the United States, left Iraq and sanctioned Iran in Ahriman's deathly stink; following the march of Constantine to Afghanistan's Kabul on this deadly ley line.

From the Gaza Strip to Pakistan's mountain heights. Cresting the frozen Himalayan heights above Islamabad this deadly ley line's corridor of war, the empathic heart tires and breaks at the thought of the suffering and all the Archonic harvests of war meted out over its 2,500-mile arc of destruction we reach the halfway point along the deadly Silk Road Ley or 1/10th Earth's diameter, reaching disputed border zone between China, Pakistan, and India.

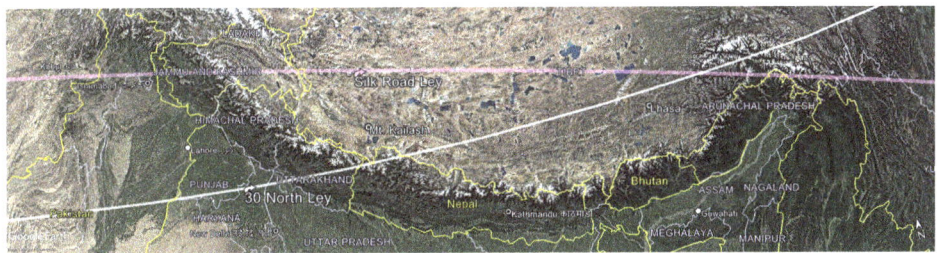

Like King Cobra around Shiva's neck the pallor of nuclear war hangs like an alpine cloud over the Himalayan heights. Quoting Bhagavad Gita and J.R. Oppenheimer, "Now I become Death, the destroyer of worlds". Crossing the Hindu Kush mountain range this ley of war enters China the autonomous region of once sovereign Tibet, in this colon like geography of the world.

Passing 100 miles south and east is the 'Abode of Shiva' Holy Mount Kailash. Regarded as sacred by Buddhist, Hindu, Jain, and Bon religions, Kailash has been a place of pilgrimage since before China's genocide of the 1.2 million Tibetans in the 1950s. A kind of library of Shiva's wisdom, this world mountain, Meru, om phallus, the axis of the cosmos; is the roof of the world. As an alignment of culture and nature, the headwaters of both the Ganga and Indus rivers are part of this dynamic focus of springing from this head of Shiva.

Shiva, the Lord of Death and renewal, shares its name with the 7-day

'Sitting Shiva' burial practices of Orthodox Jewish people 2,500 miles west in Israel. While being a God of many names and attributes, Shiva's main cause is to defeat evil wherever it is found.

While a great civilizer, the English Empire left dysfunctional societies in their wake that have polarized populations from Israel's 'Lord Ba(a)lfour Declaration' to Hong Kong at the Silk Road Ley's extreme eastern end. The fortunes made in the British opium trade, and its evil effect on Chinese and world societies was a foundational pound for London incorporated, who still profit from suffering to this day.

Also, common knowledge was the use of US Marines protecting Afghanistan's opium fields and burning others; while expediting shipments of raw opium to western opioid manufacturers, be they criminal or legal, making one ask if Hong Kong's 'Opium Wars' are still being fought to suppress the sovereign human soul-spirit.

(As a punctuation mark to today's writing, the Hamas of the Gaza Strip bombed Israel with 5000 rockets and mortar killing more than 300 inflaming this raw nerve anew.)

Every such bombing along these deadly ley lines inflamed its full length from the Mediterranean to the Pacific. On the heels of this war emotion of October 2023, a 6.3 earthquake occurred as a response of the Earth to this war emotion in Herat Afghanistan along this same deadly ley, giving testament to what Rudolf Steiner gleaned from the Akashic record that a cause and effect exists between human emotion and natural catastrophe.

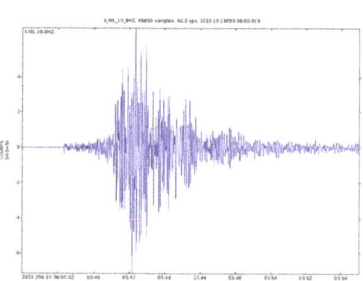

Crossing from Gaza into Israel, or from Vermont into New Hampshire, a traveler can sense a shift in the quality of place as collectively agreed upon governance and geography create tangible thought forms easily felt by the traveler. Even traversing a cornfield from Nebraska and Kansas, a sensitive soul can feel the difference. Now imagine what it's like for a mountain like Kailash to go from being in a spiritually-based theocratic Tibet to a material-based communist China. A mountain and landscape once revered as holy, doing its part to maintain the world as sacred sites do, is now regulated to the category of lifeless rock. This Abode of Shiva might not find this fits its character. The message of Shiva is; "come what may, you must never tolerate evil".

Tolerating the evil expressed by: China, Gaza, Great Britain, Israel, Iraq, Iran, India, Russia and the USA, iis surely enough to get Shiva's third eye blasting away at evil. Whether cause or effect it will be through the Abode of Shiva that healing and harmony are found on the deadly Silk Road Ley.

Continuing our overland march to the Pacific Ocean, we cross the Tibetan Plateau by Lhasa's Potala Lamas to the eastern end of the Himalayan mountain range through the disputed border of far eastern India and China. From the west to the east end of this necklace of Shiva, the Himalayas are pinned to conflict to possess its life waters.

Moving into south China, our deadly ley crosses the historically bloody landscape of Chinese Empires. Following the Xi or Pearl River to its delta this ley terminates in Hong Kong's 'fragrant harbor' of agarwood. With a history of the Opium War, and rotating possession by Britain, Japan, and China, Hong Kong is a jewel in the crown of China's south coast. The region echoes historic patterns of conflict in Israel, 5000 miles west along this deadly Silk Road Ley.

The sociopathic patterns in this deadly ley are undeniable in their repeated consistency. Dismissed as correlative by science, as no physical reason exists for its straight-line alignment of conflict, leys are seen in their effect. "known them by their works". Without consistent parties at deadly play, no single geopolitical force could be pointed to as the source of this international dissonance so apparent in its alignment.

Given the historic involvement of Britain in border design and geo-political involvement in these war zones they could be singled out. Known to profit from conflict and suffering, the usual cadre of power families, could also be pointed to as the cause behind the causal effect. Whoever or whatever may have drawn this 5000-mile line, its inflammation has become scored into spiritual dimensions. Whether cultivated to harvest human emotion by an Archonic Cloud of fear's parasites, or led by the influence of the Zarathustran demi-god of evil Ahriman to undermine the human soul, its centuries-old inflammation is habituated as a consciousness field that no one nation or people or war can resolve. Awareness of such psychopathic, sociopathic, and geopathic conditions calls for intervention.

With its dysfunction and pathology laid bare, what patterns within this disorder offer a remedy to this condition? As with all life, it's all about water or the lack thereof. Except for its passage through China, this deadly ley is all but treeless, without forest respiration to cycle and bond water to these now arid landscapes, people become naturally on edge in these precarious environments. After millennia of conquest from Alexander the Great and Mongols, as well as felling any forest for human use, made way for this desertification.

A spiritual condition remedied through spiritual dimensions demands the cooperation of Elemental forces and Nature Spirits. Set into planetary consciousness by a curse against monotheism, its transcendental supplication tends to exacerbate the problem. Given that the polytheistic Abode of Shiva is positioned at a spiritually strategic position suggests that this sacred mountain and head-water landscape is a good place to find health and freedom from this spiritual pestilence darkening the hearts of Men with the suppression of sovereign free will by the overlords of state. "Thy Will Be Done..."

Om Namah Shivaya. Side-stepping the trauma triangle of war, vengeance and savior, we let go and let God. Releasing the mantle of evil from the lands of Shiva a world tree of peace is planted, giving shade and rain over its far-reaching limbs. A tree whose roots are those of the Bodhi Tree of Buddha seen in the ridge lines radiating from this Abode of Shiva. Mount Kailash roots stretch to the canopy's edge from Israel/Palestine to Hong Kong, Taiwan, and Korea. A world tree, its trunk made of the fragrant harbor (Hong Kong) Agarwood affords tranquility to the world's mind and soul while easing inflammation and tension. A world tree rising from the roots of Mount Kailash, its peak the pinch point of a toroidal sacred Acacia tree, frames a new Ark under which a free and sovereign soul may thrive.

All the world has lived each persona of the trauma triangle along this Silk Road. Visualizing this world tree rising from the Abode of Shiva, Mount Kailash, Shiva breaks free from the Ahriman's soul-suppressing dominion into light of knowing. Looking within first "come what may, you must never tolerate evil". May goodness rain from the lands of the Acacia to the harbors of Agarwood. From the fertile fields of Ukraine and steep valleys of Korea may good reign as rain and trees grow as soul-spirits in freedom.

GREAT PYRAMID

Continuing our report on deadly ley lines affecting Middle East geopolitics our focus shifts to the eight leys radiating from the Great Pyramid as a compass rose. In its present state, a poisonous spider might be a better analogy. A geomantic case could be made that our previously explored Silk Road Ley was another projection of its noxious frequencies. Located at the center of Earth's lands, its antipode is the center of Earth's waters. Projecting the Great Pyramid, as if we see only its capstone emerging from desert sands, into the inner Earth this world pyramid's 'fire in the middle' is the Inner Core. The projection of the Pyramid's deadly ley lines traces the projection of this world pyramid to its base ring 6,000+ miles distant.

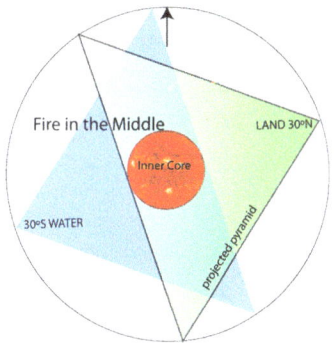

Hearkening to the days of Hollywood B movies, the likes of 'The Curse of the Mummy's Tomb' a negative view is afforded contrary to contemporary adulation of the Great Pyramid. Quoting Winston Churchill about the Russian character: with, "t's a riddle wrapped in a mystery inside an enigma...". he Great Pyramid's number, geometry, and placement have been attributed to 'Ancient Aliens' or civilizations superior to our modern era.

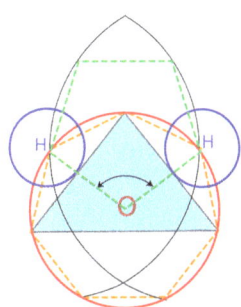

Not a treatise on the Great Pyramid form and number we leave those remunerations to the cadre of searchers who make it their reason for being. This author's contribution to pyramid thinking was the observation of its apex angle being that of the bonding angle of water— bonding this construct to the Earth's water filled biosphere. Bonded as such, its pyramidal worldview is set into planetary consciousness as a model for top-down control by priesthood and kingdoms who would, like Ahriman, enslave humanity below.

The suppression and control of humanity's free will has been an age-old problem to those who would attempt to hold dominion over these sovereign ensouled beings, "who's your daddy." A case can be made that evil arises from the exercise of free will by an 'I' and 'ego' separated from the full knowledge of Creation. It is this control dynamic that infects the Great Pyramid's deadly ley lines over those who would resist the will of the Other. With this in mind, we begin our journey into the darkness of this curse of the mummy's tomb.

Digging deep into past, present and future what follows is a chronicle of the Great Pyramids eight ley lines that has formed a world wide web, capturing all in a deadly struggle of sovereignty versus control.

On the Road to Mecca

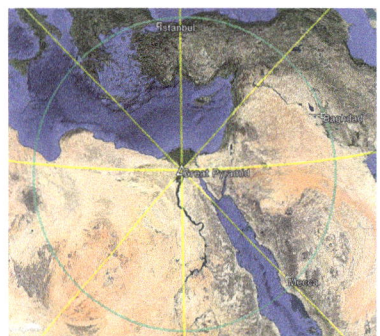

The shortest overland Great Pyramid ley, its southeast ley line is perhaps the most significant as it points to the Kaaba of Mecca, 800 miles distant across the Red Sea. Marking a radius centered on the Great Pyramid the Mecca ley arcs to encompass both Baghdad and Istanbul in a ring of Islam that includes the Levant and then some. In geomantic metaphor, Allah's lunar god Kabba in orbiting this pyramidal model of the earth affects the tides within its greater hidden temple complex.

Esoteric and physical science has an upshot of earth energy emitting as a fountain from the Great Pyramid. Grounding this torus donut-like loop the ancient Kemet placed an obelisk to ground its power at the temple entrance. Precisely placed, the Kaaba grounds the pyramid, generating an 800-mile radial torus field tuned to Islam.

Entering the sacred grounds of the Kaaba through the marble arc of Hateem/Hijr Ismail this ley was likely worked by pre-Islamic pagans who worshiped the Moon God, Allah, at this site. While called the religion of peace, it is a matter of historical record and doctrine that Islam was spread by the sword. For this reason, this ley is one of the Earth's most violent and deadly ley lines for its intolerance of any non-Islamic relationship with God. A clearly deadly pyramidal worldview.

Transversing Saudi Arabia, this deadly ley continues through war-torn Yemen, and Somali Horn of Africa, and across the Indian Ocean to the ocean's southeast where the world pyramid surfaces near 49S 119E

North by North West

Turning back from Mecca to the Great Pyramid we look northwest along another deadly ley along the west edge of the Nile Delta fan to Alexandria, Egypt to Italy, France's Brittany, to its endpoint of the world pyramid edge in the State of Durango, Mexico.

A world matrix with many geophysical planes oriented to the Great Pyramid. The Nile Delta's fan points to the Giza, as does the Nile River. Italy's boot points there, as do African and Palestinian coastlines. There is only one other place on earth where such geophysical planes point and that is Shelburne Falls, Massachusetts; the geologic center of the North American tectonic plate. The book Gaia Matrix expands on this center-point relationship with North America.

In effect, when French Muslims pray towards Mecca their supplications are filtered through Italy and the Great Pyramid, grounding with head to earth Islam to France and Europe in an ever increasing orbit of intolerance.

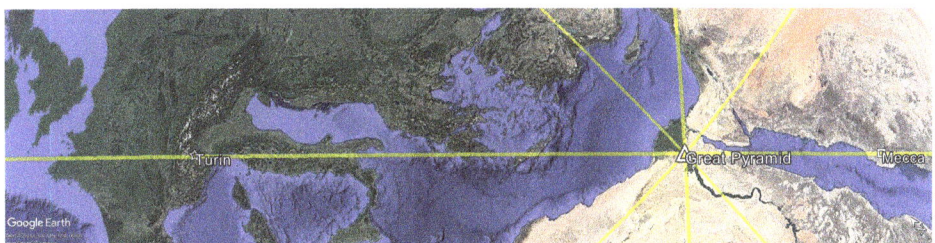

It bears mentioning that faith, however far from the truth, when focused by the collective consciousness in an agreed-upon subservience of individual free will to a collective faith-based will, miraculous things happen. Along this Northwest deadly ley, we find Turin, Italy where the Shroud of Turin has received so much adoration that the light of Christ shines through this burial shroud, be it real or a bogus relic. With the rise of secularism and freedom of the individual in Italy and France, the group focus and agreed-upon worldview of Islam fills the vacuum with its fervent belief in and adherence to the Koran.

Transceiving through this deathly worldview and pyramidal edifice, any Muslim's prayers for peace will without a doubt be corrupted and hijacked by the dark lords of the pyramid to its opposite manifestation—a religion of peace spread by war.

Following the burning of the Library of Alexandria, Christian zealots deprived the world of its history with deathly repeated histories to follow. Along this Northwest Ley, through the ancient kingdom of Sparta and Italy's Roman Empire war, was a way of life. From the arc of Italy's boot, we give a wave to Spartacus and his fellow crucified rebel slaves. The pyramid's wave of death swept over Roman lands with successive conquest; with its Holy Roman Empire as barbarous as any barbarian invader in their pursuit of profit from the suffering of others.

Like an arrow from the dark lords controlling the pyramid, this Northwest Ley arcs over the Italian and French peninsulas of Brittany in a straight line over the North Atlantic Ocean. Making landfall in Maritime Canada through the Saint Lawrence fault zone tearing North America in two. But before we take the Titanic westward let us take a more in-depth look at this Deadly ley through Europe and the Mediterranean.

In the geologic maelstrom of tectonic forces, this northwest deadly ley first crosses Crete after leaving continental Africa. At the head of the Minotaur horn of islands, connecting Greece to Turkey, Crete has hosted civil and world wars, Minoan king's rule, and spats between the Venetian and Ottoman wannabe rules of the indomitable peoples in its liminal space between here and there. In these mythic waters of Ulysses and Jason, and the blast zone of Santorini volcano, ancient Crete has opposed the forces of the dark over-lordship of the pyramidal worldview.

Then there are the 23+ wars fought by Sparta between 700-189 BC that made for a warrior's cult on that Greek Island. Following its ley trajectory through, all that is Italy, we cross the Alps into France within 20 miles of CERN.

Well within the waveform meander of this ley CERN, whose ring's geometry echoes that of the Great Pyramid spin the atomic forces to destruction in pursuit of the god-particle. In search of a material god, scientists experiment with mini 'black holes' to view the spiritual forces of the universe. It brings to mind the Vietnam War adage: "we had to destroy the village to save it". Its atom smasher machine is in the geometry of an 'Einstein Ring'. Accused of altering space-time by its untold side effects, CERN caused a 'Mandela Effect' where timelines split as divergent memory.

Hard to forget, the memory of French: wars, revolutions and Napoleons has fertilized its soil with the blood of patriots along this deadly ley.

Approaching the coast of Brittany we find fortified Ste Malo(bad), the causeway to island of Mount Saint Michael and distant Saint Michael

Island off England's Land End. At these places we find honor in the name and statue Archangel Michael, who gives his all to put down the evil worm under foot. With his meteoric iron sword Archangel Michael is seen as a counterforce to this great adversary who would enslave and suppress the spiritually evolving free will of humanity.

Crossing the WWII naval war zone of the North Atlantic; following lengthy fault splits we cross the stretch marks of the Mid-Atlantic Rift. Through Newfoundland and now southwest along the plane of the St Lawrence River fault zone we enter into the centuries old divide between English and French Canada. A plane of the historic conflict, this all but straight 300-mile St. Lawrence River's path of this deadly ley crosses the war and ship wreck waters lakes Ontario and Erie, to the Mississippi River confluence with the Ohio River at New Madrid Seismic Zone.

Not limited to human violence, this deadly ley's passage through the New Madrid fault zone rumbled to life in 1811 when a 9.2 earthquake made the Mississippi flow north and subsided the land in the shape of a big foot. Pre-colonial Natives might say, this footprint was that of the creator being Hobbamock who brings good and evil to life. This quake even toppled chimneys in Maine.

In 1811, there were no cities in its immediate seismic zone. If, and when, another such quake occurs nearby Memphis, Tennessee, we will have more than Elvis to mourn. New Madrid, at the heart of America, is on the Missouri Compromise latitude dividing North and South leading to the U.S. Civil War, a divide that still exists as state borders today. Also a geologic divide, the geologic plutons rising beneath New Madrid will in time open a waterway from Quebec City to New Orleans. It was around this geographic divide of people, place and purpose that the five routes eastern tribes walked and starved in their 'Trail of Tears' on a forced relocation to the Indian Territories of Oklahoma. A focus point of the sins of America New Madrid is emblematic as a "source of a river" of blood sacrificed for a Nation made of all the world's peoples.

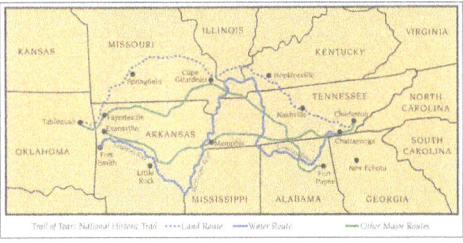

A deadly ley line in deed and word, its passage is scored through Texas in memory of the Alamo, where legendary Davy Crockett fought the Mexican army nearly single-handedly; like some Spartan hero at Thermopylae. The irony is not lost that the battle for the Alamo was

fought over illegal immigration into Mexico by American colonials. Moving into Mexico our passage of death is completed in the violent drug cartel-controlled Durango Mexico; one of four points of the world pyramid on dry land.

Completing the Great Pyramid's northwest arc of deadly ley from Giza capstone to Mexico cornerstone this edge of our world pyramid wielded influence over the European and North American experience. Countering emperor and adversary's controlling force through Alexandria, quanta breaching CERN, and Cartel drug labs of Mexico; Archangel Michael fights the good fight for goodwilled freedom across this world of joy and sorrows.

Following this ley across North America and Mexico, the Great American Ecplise of April 2024 overshadowed its passage, with a hoped for cosmic reset of this deadly ley, as a harmonizing effect to pyramid's dissonant frequency.

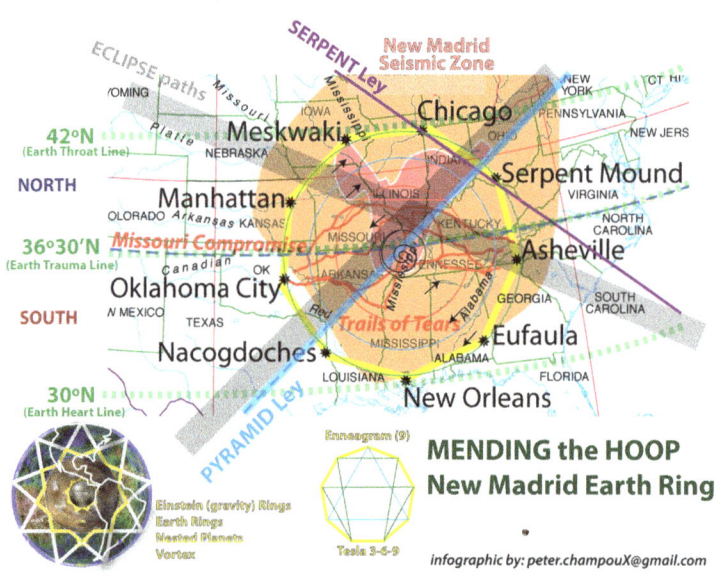

Latitude with Attitude

Returning to the center via the 30th N—latitude with the attitude—the observer, of this worldwide trauma triad of victim, bully, and hero, makes a return visit to The Alamo eastward by New Orleans' Mississippi Delta through Morocco, Algeria, Libya, and Egypt to the Nile Delta and the Great Pyramid's western door to the world.

Exiting its eastern door into the warring Middle East and Asia our 30th N latitude deltas the Tigris-Euphrates and Yangtze rivers while sourcing the Ganges, Indus, and Brahmaputra rivers. Coursing near Mount Kailash (already indicated), located on 31N.

One might equate the 30th to a planetary heart line as this is where Earth's blood, or water, flows to and from. At the northern limits of the subtropical Coriolis Effect, the 30th North latitude water flows are the effects of this vortex dynamic generated by atmospheric drag on Earth's spin.

On an anthropomorphized Earth, the 30th would correlate to the Heart or fourth chakra. To continue this analogy the Arctic Circle would be its Crown and Earth Core its root chakra. The Goldilocks zone of civilization of the 40s gives voice, while the 19.5 N is the planet's solar plexus of volcanic navels and the Equator's Amazon and Congo rivers its Sacral center of passion. It is thought in the religious text that Man was made in the image and likeness of God—like all of creations' glory.

In its state of ruin, the Great Pyramid expresses itself as the broken heart of the world. Stripped of its casing stone in the 1303 Crete Earthquake, contemporary to the 1305 demise of the Knights Templar, its stones were carted away to build Cairo. Today, the picture of entropy, the Great Pyramid tunes Earth's heart with dissonance. It sides at a 51.51 degree angle and the Great Pyramid's apex angle at 103.02 degrees the pyramid bonds to the biosphere like water's hydrogen bonds to oxygen. Presently, as the result of its missing casement, the pyramid angle reflects the polluted condition of contemporary earth waters. Serving as a bonding mechanism for both Earth's waters and that of Man, the pyramid's entropy is expressed in the entropic state of top-down governance and the disintegrating bonds between people at war along the pyramid's deadly ley lines.

From east to west the Great Pyramid bonds to world delta waters in the seven sacred directions as a strategic artifact so placed as to have the greatest influence of the Earth's field of consciousness. Perhaps beneficial when first built, this pyramid has degenerated and may have been spiritually hijacked by Dark Forces, as seen in the effects of its radiating carnage. Awareness and acknowledgement of its influence on Earth's ill health and war agnist itself may just be the first step on Earth's path to recovery, free of its deadly influence that has taken control of this Heart of the World.

NORTH to KYIV

Having just toured 30N, by the coincidence of placement, the Great Pyramid is also on the 30th longitude coursing north-south through what is termed geographically, the Nile Meridian. This meridian divides the African continent east and west along the caduceus of the Nile River. From the 30,00-year-old 'Adam's Calendar' of South Africa, through the great Sudd Swamp of warring South Sudan the Nile Meridian crosses the Great Pyramid and apex of the Nile's fan-like delta north to Turkey the Black Sea, dividing Ukraine in two.

Where a latitude delineated environmental zones based on the ecliptic Sun exposure, longitude measures time, the fourth dimension. Set and primed by Greenwich, England, time as a cultural construct is lorded over by the British political system, Darwinian economics, and the world language of business. A very neat British construct to have the pyramid exactly 30 degrees east of its Prime Meridian thus subsuming it as part of its 12-beat (30/360=12) system of time.

As arbitrary as the measurement of time, borders between countries are as fickle as the revolving tyrants of the day. One day it's Ottoman Turks and the next Royal British geographers, ensuring ongoing border disputes followed by the post-World War II Soviet Union. For some reason, described by war's historians, the western border of Russia with the Soviet Bloc states is along the Nile Meridian, except for Ukraine. Dividing Ukraine in half it appears to the Russian Putin's intent to continue this western boundary along the 30th East. A country that spans nearly halfway around the world, its geopolitical integrity as a viable country is dependent upon possession of the eastern half of Ukraine and Crimea's waterways and gas pipelines into the Sea of Azov.

As an identity, the Rus sense of self can be traced to Kyiv, the spiritual heart of the Russian Orthodox Religion. Dividing the world in polarity, north south east and west, the Nile Meridian tuned to the discordant frequency of the Great Pyramid sets up Ukraine as the battleground between Russia and NATO. Multilingual speaking Odessa, Ukraine just west of the 30th east longitude is a testament to this divide. Splitting the world as it split the atom in the Chernobyl nuclear reactor meltdown, this Great Pyramid deadly ley, if ignored as an effect, will lead to a greater war of dominion.

Drawing out the Nile Meridian to its full extent of the world pyramid, the 30th crosses the North Pole and the oil fields of Prudhoe Bay, following the Alaska Pipeline through Fairbanks, Alaska, and witnessed the Valdez oil spill before ending in the Pacific Ocean some 8000 miles distant from desert pyramid.

Coursing south following the Nile, meandering through the genocide and ethnic cleansing zones of South Sudan, Uganda, and Rwanda; this meridian strings the bow of the Great Rift Valley's arc of lakes. Passing through the ancestral lands of Australopithecus Lucy, the 30th meridian highlights Ruwa, Zimbabwe where a schoolyard of children witnessed a UFO land and were greeted by ET beings in odd clothes. Continuing through Great Zimbabwe, Adam's Calendar, and long-suffering South Africa this southern meridian of the world pyramid terminates in mysterious Antarctica.

The litany of conflict and polluted landscapes arrayed around the Great Pyramid is answered in polarity. Confronted with man's war-tuned strings, the world harp oscillates the Nile, Great Rift Valley, and Great Pyramid sounds like fingernails across a chalkboard.

Continuing with our correlative metaphor as a spiritual science, the strings (leys) of the Great Pyramid are out of tune, resounding as trauma across its Compass Rose.

In a fret of untuned discord, the 30th E Nile Meridian tunes the other 7 strings of the pyramid's octave. This meridian's Nile and Great Rift valleys give shape to a string-tuned waveform of polar electromagnetism. For lack of a turn-key to fit the Great Pyramid, tuning our world harp, verily, is sounding more like a screaming Bigfoot, than a tabernacle choir praising Creation.

Busted like a rock star's guitar, the Great Pyramid tuned world harp strings are dissonant—tuning key, fret, soundboard, and armature to pluck. Short of restoring the Great Pyramid to its original time place and perfected state...other methods are needed.

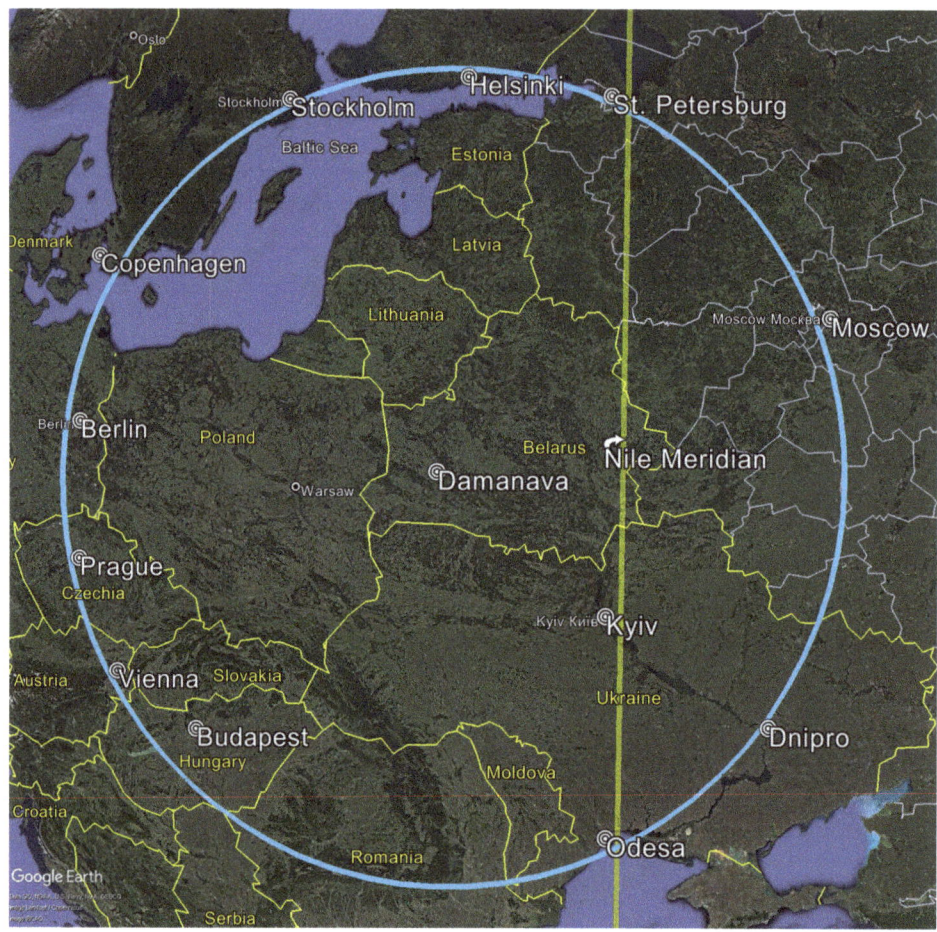

A 'sounding board' made of northern Europe high culture cities, Odessa and St. Petersburg pluck the Nile Meridian with concordant resonant philharmonic (to-love-harmony) play. Curving south and west along the Carpathian mountains to Vienna, Prague, and Berlin a philharmonic cacophony of its 'ring song'. Clockwise northward around the Baltic Sea's west coast through Copenhagen, Stockholm, Helsinki, and St. Petersburg; our 1000 mile diameter 'sounding board' keys Nile Meridian to a higher octave of philharmonic tuned 'resonance' sounding Great Pyramid strung world harp.

Hermetics suggests; "change frequency to change the manifestation of mass". The violent, life-defying manifestation of mass trauma on the Great Pyramid's deadly frequency change is called for.

Its discordant world-view pumping up the egos of despots, the Great

Pyramid's geo(ego)magnetic charged telluric Nile Meridian would divide 'us' from 'them'. Assuming throne atop the peasant dead below, the impetus towards the oneness of social good will has been co-opted by the will of world despots. Once the world meridian that tuned time to the harmonizing frequency of water the Nile runs red with the curse of Moses against Pharaoh. "Let My People Go", you dark heart of the world.

X Marks the Spot

Crossing the Great Pyramid in a world spaning X from Northeast to Southwest, curving over Earth to far Pacific 8000 miles distant the Pyramid's NE deadly ley links the Giza plateau with deadly Wake and atomic Bikini islands.

Called the Alamo of the Pacific, the Battle of Wake Island was the first battle fought by the USA in WWII following the Pearl Harbor, Hawaii attack by Japanese forces. Fought from December 8, 1941, to December 23, 1941, was a demonstration of American grit to the attacking Japanese and a morale booster for Americans to git-er-done. It was in these Marshall Islands that the U.S. tested 46 nuclear weapons between 1946 and 1958 explosively, setting these anti-life frequencies in the beauty of Bikini Island base of the World Pyramid.

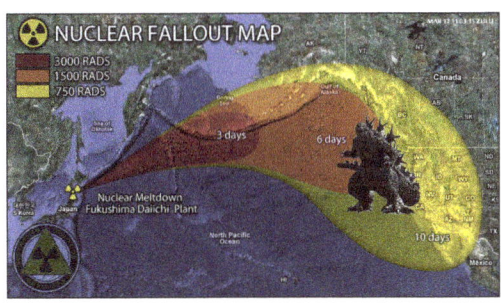

Drawn ever westward across radioactive waters, the dimension-shifting demon Godzilla stomps Fukushima Nuclear Power Plant with tsunami foot as it makes its way to djinn home of the Great Pyramid. Fording nuclear Japan, the ley crosses the Sea of Japan to the three-nation border zone along the Teman River between North Korea, China, and Russia. Following the broad stroke of Mongol conquest through Manchuria and northern Mongolia to the four-nation border point of where Russia, Mongolia, China, and Kazakhstan meet near the Denisovan Caves of the Altai Mountains.

A convergence point of geographies, the Denisovan Altai caves served as home for hominids long before the Great Pyramids. Dating to 50,000 BCE, dating in the warmth of this cave between hominid species is evidenced in DNA remains. One such remains was the Denisovan tooth, a much, much larger tooth than all others found in its successive layers of habitation. Bigfoot country!

At the most northerly point of the Pyramid's northeast deadly ley, from the Altai convergence, we enter the nuclear bomb testing zone of Kazakhstan and Uzbekistan with oil fields to dried up the Aral Sea. An echo of the Marshall Island nuclear testing, the Soviets detonated 456 nuclear bombs at Kazakistan's Semipalatinsk-21 test site known as "The Polygon". Yet another strident footfall of a nuclear Godzilla across Asia to the Middle East, our deadly ley crosses the oily Caspian Sea. Caspian, the sea god of power, life, and chaos, is a might felt by Armenia on the sea's western shore.

Ascribed as the cradle of modern civilization, Armenia has been considered a holy place of origin by ancient Sumerians and Egyptians. The geography of Armenia is another confluence of nations with Turkey, Russia, and Iran coveting this jewel. Known for their wisdom the Armenian people have threatened yet necessary to ruling elite. A Christian culture, Armenia has been nearly squeezed out of existence by neighboring Muslims. From 1915-1919, the Young Turk of the Ottoman Empire defined the term genocide in their treatment of Armenians when between one and ten million were killed, tortured, and starved as yet another deadly event along this ley.

Called Eden by some, Armenia, at the source of Tigris-Euphrates and the landing site of Noah's Ark on Mount Ararat, gives place to a long-held sacred relationship coveted by those who would possess its land for legitimacy. Under the boot heel of pyramidal tyranny, the Land of Aram is an example to all those who would underestimate the cruelty and deprivations found along this deadly ley line. In a forced march into the eastern Syria desert, the Armenia diaspora was but a prelude to what followed over the next hundred years worldwide in the shadow of the Great Pyramid.

With increasing speed and ferocity, we enter Kurdistan, left out of the British redesign of the Ottoman Empire. The Kurds as a people, were left with no place to call home. Resulting in endless conflict permanently destabilizing the region, successive generations of Kurds dream of a home as ethnic orphans in diaspora throughout Turkey, Iran, Iraq, and Syria.

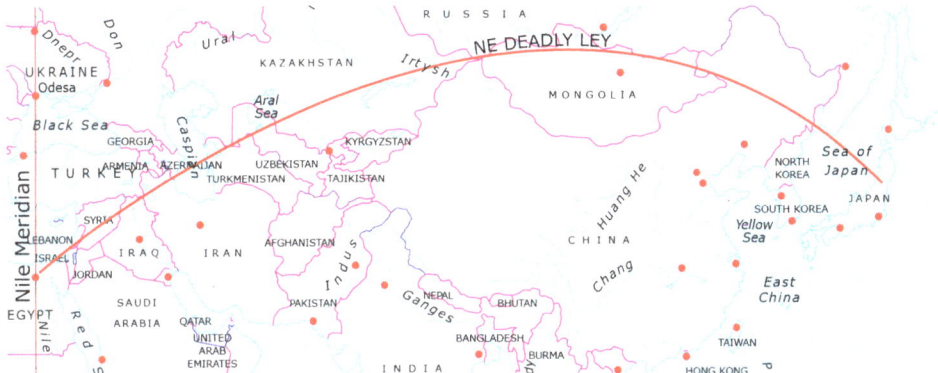

Stomping through Syria, one city after another, Godzilla has laid yet another country to waste under the banner of "there is no god, ..." while acting as gods themselves, determining life and death for the innocent or guilty, as if in full knowledge of Love's will. A twelve-year civil war in stalemate, its only effect has been the diaspora of another 13 million from home, tribe, religion, nation, and life. A war between acronyms, started by the torture and killing of young graffiti artist, and one 'Arab Spring' by yet another divinely ordained regime. Spawning the likes of ISIL and ISIS, the desert djinn hatred of mankind called in a rain of demi-god fire upon Syria from USA and other aggrandizing acronyms.

Stepping over the ruin upon ancient ruin, fresh with death's stench, we pass Paul on the road to Damascus and question...what's up...pointing to the one truth that covers all. Passing through this oldest capital city in the world, Damascus has been conquered successively by armies of Assyria, Babylon, Persia, Greece, Rome, Ottoman, and French since its inception 6,000 years ago around its desert oasis.

If not for war, history books would have little to report. A driver of invention, war and its death seems to be in the fabric of the world. Caused by the devil without or the one within, the trauma triangle of war seen as an observer gives perspective to its causes. As the reader approaches the contested border of Israel, another confluence of borders is crossed into Mount Hermon and the Golan Heights. This border continues along the Lebanon border into the Plains of Armageddon of northern Israel for more history of war and religion, so prevalent along the Great Pyramid's deadly ley lines.

Before crossing the azure Mediterranean Sea to the Suez Canal, Cairo, and Great Pyramid we pause on the slopes of Mount Carmel by the sea to reflect upon our journey to the Holy Land. OK, that's enough reflecting let's get back to our tragic play on the pathos of human sacrifice.

The first site of historic and religious significance after this deadly ley exits the Pyramid and Nile Delta, Mount Carmel looms large on the horizon of war. First mentioned in the Old Testament, Mount Carmel was the site of a 9th century BCE spiritual battle between Elijah, backed by (the one and only god) Yahweh, and 450 prophets of that pagan human sacrifice god Baal, aka El, to prove whose God was greatest; setting the tone for this deadly ley line.

The setup was that the adherents were required to have their altar sacrificed oxen consumed by divine fire. After days of trying, the prophets of Baal gave up in despair, only to have Elijah set the poor animal ablaze at first try. Ending a prolonged drought it began to rain extinguishing the blaze, all 450 loser priests of Baal were killed and Baal became a footnote of history living on in epigenetic memory of human sacrifice over whose god is greater. Allah-Hu-Akbar!

Like a sieve screen or filter through which the northeast Great Pyramid's ley passes, the spiritual and material memories held by Mount Carmel set the tone for this inflamed nerve of the world. Like the lightning strike rain making Elijah called forth from Yahweh, this lightning strike burns the sacrificed with weapons of mass destruction.

Mount Carmel's commanding heights tower over the Bay of Acre, forming the southern arc of Israel's one harbor. Across the bay from Carmel is the old city of Acre, the commandery of the Knights Templar for their three Crusades for the Holy Land. It was from here the Knights Templar and Christian forces were sent packing by Saladin the Magnificent at the end of the last Crusade.

This second filter or template of war was set in place by Templar magus and repeated by Napoleon in 1799. A case could be made for a third filter of war is the Israeli navy base in nearby Haifa.

Those with the third eye to see, report that the Great Pyramid is an amplifier. Intuitives witness that collective thought forms, like those of war, are taken in, amplified and returned in ever-increasing waves of emotions of the trauma triangle of war. Reversing these emotions of war transmitted through the pyramid's deadly ley it is suggested they be replaced by the emotions of: life, love, and soul sovereignty.

Monotheism is another such frequency cycling through and being amped up by the Great Pyramid. While earlier in our study the Kaaba of Mecca was on its southeast edge ley, here we find on the slopes of Mount Carmel the Baha'i and Carmelite religious order. Religion is often cited as the cause of war and the opioid of the masses. Contrary to the polytheism espoused by ancient Egyptians and the indigenous sovereign relationships between soul and Creatrix, monotheism demands one form to the exclusion of all other forms of monotheism. Ask any Native American about this.

Ameliorating the entrained cycles of war and religious intolerance, the Bahá'í Shrine and religious center predominantly placed on Mount Carmel, through the surreptitious hand of Grace, is an impulse towards peace and tolerance on this deadly ley line.

"Bahá'í beliefs address such essential themes as the oneness of God and religion, the oneness of humanity and freedom from prejudice, the inherent nobility of the human being, the progressive revelation of religious truth, the development of spiritual qualities, the integration of worship and service, the fundamental equality of the sexes, the harmony between religion and science, the centrality of justice to all human endeavors, the importance of education, and the dynamics of the relationships that are to bind together individuals, communities, and institutions as humanity advances towards its collective maturity."

Unfortunately, the Bahá'í influence has been compromised by the architects of its Shrine of the Bab' on Mount Carmel as its focusing staircase to the shrine's mount does not orient to its prophet's resting place in Acre or in enneagonal (9) alignment with the North and the world.

The reason why this shrine is located here is, in a large part, due to its proximity to the Ottoman prison colony, where Bahá'í prophet

Baha'u'llah was imprisoned for much of his life In geomantic metaphor, the positive ethics, espoused by the faith, are unfortunately imprisoned by the wars and religions that surround it.

Leaving the last 8000 miles and 8000 years of suffering of both humanity and Earth in the orchards of Mount Carmel, we complete the crossing of our X as we cross the Nile and see what emotional impulses are being transmitted to the pyramid from the southwest for an increase of amplitude.

Wakefull to the destructive force of both atom and Adam the fallen condition of the world as portrayed by this deadly ley of the Great Pyramid gives one great pause. Man's inhumanity to Man is laid bare in the desert wastes of Syria along this world miasma of war. Tempered by the suffering and God aligned will of prophets the demise of the Ottoman caliphate soon followed. With a bell rung from Mount Carmel heights the message of unity and a call to prayer is heard to change the dissonance in both pyramid and Man.

South by West

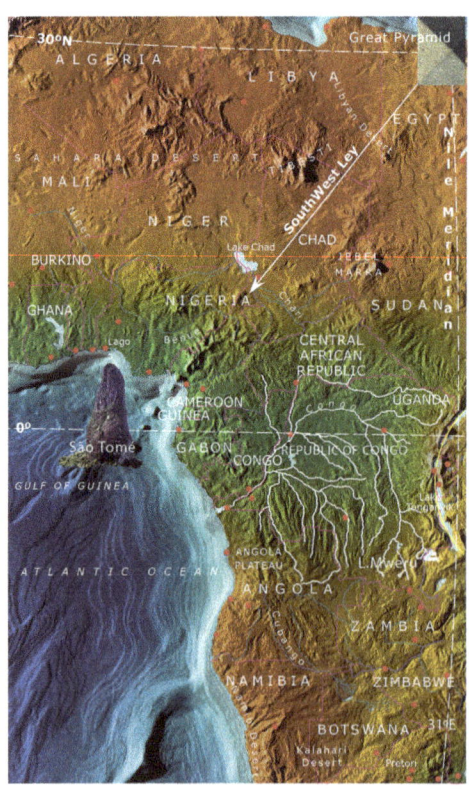

Earlier in our narrative, it was described how the upshooting pyramidal earth energies were grounded through an obelisk, generating an electromagnetic loop or donut-like field that circulates through the heart and Earth. In the old English/Alantian system of telluric enhancement for agricultural benefit a stone circle, or Medicine Wheel, was placed instead of a pyramid, and a megalithic monolith was placed as a grounding obelisk. This repeating pattern of circle and monolith generated a multi-dimensional undulating etheric stream of vitalizing forces to whatever input was set as intention.

While the Great Pyramid had many obelisk grounding rods, as a world pyramid its grounding obelisk is found to its southwest aligned to a volcanic string of vents in distant Atlantic coastal waters of Cameroon. Along this line of archipelago islands in the Gulf of Guinea is its largest island Sao Tome or Saint Thomas. Named as such for the island's 663 m high finger, Cao Grande (Great Canine), this obelisk of the world pyramid satisfies Thomas' doubts. Marking the radius of the Great Pyramids, its etheric loop is completed spanning the breadth of Africa.

In the early 1970's, a solar storm sparked a display of northern lights seen from Canada to Louisiana. Called the "eye of god", this light phenomena starts with a point at zenith that extends as a line to the horizon. Adding one waving line after another from zenith to horizon it expanded as a fan for 355 degrees until only a circle at the center and a single missing line remained in its shimmering red glow at twilight. This is what might be visualized as the pattern generated between the Great Pyramid eye/zenith and Cao Grande obelisk/horizon.

Fans of 'The Hobbit' might equate this pyramid to Sauron's great eye atop its tower in Mordor scanning and enslaving all from its perch at the middle of earth's landmasses. Awakening the enslaved to this controlling dark overlord is offered more to free than condemn human beings struggling with right-use of free will.

The deadly ley line projected from the southwest edge of the Great Pyramid to the full extent of its world pyramid spans 8000 miles, from the South Atlantic Ocean to the southern Falkland Islands of South America. Crossing mostly deserts and oceans this ley's death cult was most fully expressed in the slave trade of West Africans.

Practicioners of human sacrifice to appease deities or slaver African tribal warlords and kings, served Ahriman in their unique way. However, the trophy for African mega-death along this ley goes to King Leopold II of Belgium, who presided over the deaths of 15 million of the Congo's native peoples from 1885 to 1908. The cruelty used in Leopold's efforts to advance his profits from the Congo was as staggering as it was creative.

It gives one pause to think what accomplishments could have been made by those burned in world war altars of human sacrifice for profit and god.

The direct focus of Sauron's gaze on this deadly ley is upon Cameroon, Chad, and Darfur—all experiencing death, atrocities, and diaspora of refugees in their silent genocidal civil war—a breath of expanding emotion through ley and pyramid. To quote the shortest sentence in the bible, "Jesus wept" for Africa with agape love.

The bounds of this middle earth are like the deadly ley lines that crisscross, with one example after another of inhumanity around its circumference. Just as wind is only known by its effects, the patterns of destruction are also an invisible spiritual force upon a material world. Yes, correlative reasoning is not a valid line of inquiry in the material world, but is valid in spiritual science. What is it about, this pile of stones that geology, religious centers, and genocides point to other than a mirror for Man? What is the nature of this mirror, is it a machine gone rogue, a portal to Hades? An instrument as crucible for soul growth?

What are these Great Pyramids, and why are they a focus point of destruction? We see how they rest at a latitude of the heart, where rivers flow to and from. Perhaps the rivers of blood flow through this heart of the world for the same reasons. They are fed by death cult religious doctrine of top-down dominance, with a mandate to elevate one over the 'other' as does the geometry of the pyramid.

Named by the Greek visitors, the pyramids looked like pyramis, a Greek pastry. Also named pyramidos by the Greek visitors meaning 'fire in the middle', speaks to the pyramid's white fire-like form in the desert sun.

The Egyptians themselves called a pyramid "mer", and the Great Pyramids the Horizon of Khufu. Mer being the spinning light of God, within the body KA on the soul BA—the merkaba.

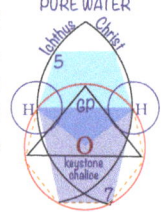

We have seen how the 51.51-degree angle and 103.2 apex angle are the bonding angle of hydrogen to oxygen. Hydrogen, as we know, burns as the sun. Perhaps hydrogen is the fire in the middle alluded to by Greek argonauts. Ra or sun worshiping the power of solar hydrogen, seeks to bond to air, and oxygen, via its geometry.

Awakening from the miasma of curses that seemingly spawned millennia of religious and world wars, man needs
to let God be god, and up aside his nuclear power over creation before there is no Earth to steward. A reversal is seen as necessary. Knowing of their existence, deadly ley lines will gradually become lively leys when we as humanity stop falling into their trap.

The Great Pyramids are not inherently evil; they simply amplify whatever is input from the emotional field of the biosphere. Just as the emotions of the trauma triangle ever increase as it cycles through the horizons of mer, so can the emotions of love be increased and expanded upon.

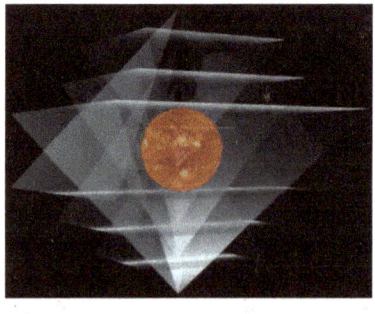

Spinning a Merkaba to heal the Mer of Egypt and its attendant leys, one attempts to bring together the two bases of a mer that are of the same polarity. When we try to push two negative or positive ends of a magnetic together, they repulse each other in its torsion field. Drawing two mirrored mer together, along an axis, they spin in opposite directions at ever-increasing speed as their bases get closer until they can not get any closer. At this maximum point of magnetic non-polarity a light, a mer, is ignited at its middle. So lit by two water bonds a stream of liquid light of love is seen circulating through these deadly leys, clearing the trauma of the ages, transforming the heart of the world with leys enliven with its ambrosia.

42°NORTH LATITUDE, The Dream of Empire

Shifting from dunes to mountain ranges, our search for the cause behind the cause for the deadly nature of not only these ley lines but this planet of sorrows in total. Every border drawn was fought or is being fought and hacked over until what has become the geography of Earth. One might conclude, due to the prevalence of war, that a line could be drawn in any direction and multiple wars would be found. A bandwidth that aligns with 42nd North latitude is a Goldilocks zone on this Goldilocks third planet from the sun that imperialists covet.

The Great Pyramid was found situated on the 30th latitude heart chakra line because of the rivers that flowed to and from this latitude, like blood to and from the heart. The 42nd's qualities and relative position could be called the Earth's fifth or Throat Chakra. More a band width that spans 40 to 45 degrees north latitude, this deadly necklace is the choke collar of Empire. From the Chinese Empire in the Far East, to the American Empire in the Far West, this deadly ley has brought some of the greatest blood and the greatest light of high culture. The finest art and most illumined thought to the world.

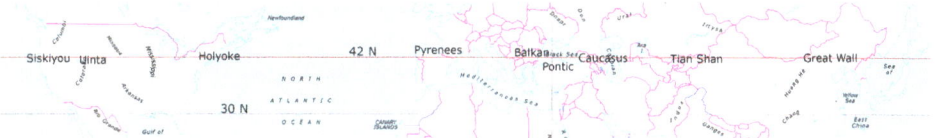

In retrospect, it is a favored latitude for this itinerant author from his birth in Massachusetts, to residence in Michigan, to college in Utah, to fatherhood in Oregon. The home of Saint Francis of Assisi and Genghis Khan, the 42nd has hosted great universities and appropriation of holy wisdom's Lady of Light. Bulging like an Adam's Apple. and a vertebrae of the world, along this latitude are found the transverse mountain ranges of the world and the Great Wall of China in a circumferential environmental zone where humanity's death cry to Creator and mother echoes through heights and valleys.

Traveling east to west, in the advance of empire, we move clockwise against Earth's spin. With each stride giving motion to the world as we push off one foot to the next with the stride of armies and gallop of calvary's stead.

Paddling through the flotsam of the storm-wrecked Mongol in the Sea of Japan the 42nd comes to shore at the shores of the Russian, North Korean, and China border, where we learned the Great Pyramid's dead ley passed. Striding into the Chinese mainland its well-known history of warlords and emperors is documented in a millennia

of history. The dividing line between Manchuria and Southern China the "forbidden" City of Heaven in Beijing has presided over shifting rulership for centuries to the present day where the People's Republic of China who orchestrated cultural purges that eliminated the nation's brain trust leaving Genghis Khan's gene pool to rule as 'Gang of Four' and Xi

Heading west the guard towers of China's come into view. Like a dragon across imperial China, the Great Wall was attributed to the first emperor of China Qin Shi Huang. Uniting existing walls erected to slow northern invaders, Haung completed it as construct on Earth in 220+ BCE. Also known as the world's largest graveyard it was estimated that over the 2,000 years it took to complete 400,000 to 500,000 died in its construction, whose bodies were used as fill behind rampart walls. Even Huang's architect for the project is said to have committed suicide over the wall's negative effect on the flow of chi southward.

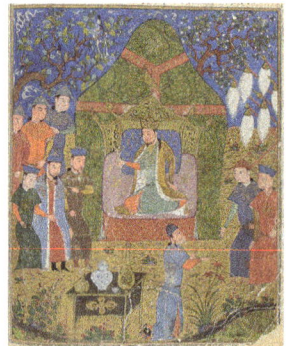
China's most prolific and expendable resource, its long-suffering humanity has long been its building block in war and peace. Counting only the dead of China along this deadly ley line, it's already looking like the necklace worn by the Hindu goddess of death Kali. China's "Queen Mother of the West ', goddess of death, Xiwangmu would approve. An impulse Genghis Khan's Mongol hoarders were all too willing to oblige across the broad steps of western China in their dream of empire.

Moving at Earth's rotational speed of 770 mph along the 42nd, a sonic boom is heard coming from Kyrgyzstan's throat singing. The human throat chakra has been depicted as a kind of trumpet horn. At China's far western border, we find the mountainous country of Kyrgyzstan, itself shaped like a trumpet with a mouthpiece in the east and a bell sounding the 42nd in its west. Made of 88 (octave) ranges its main mountain chain is the Tian Shan, the celestial "mountains of heaven" sounds the Horde's arrival in the stans.

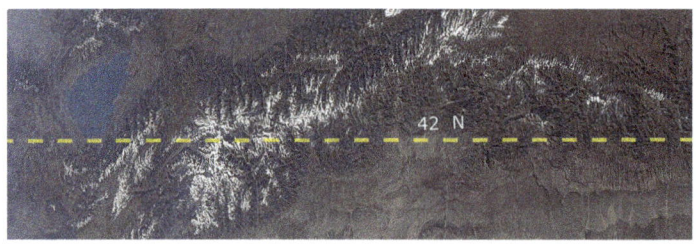

A source of mountain fresh waters to a parcher land, Kyrgyzstan has had 52 wars during its 2200-year history. A paltry sum given the 107 wars the United States fought, mostly against its native peoples, during its 250 years of curative bloodletting.

From the Land of Kyrgyz, we scream at 770 mph across the stan, the place of Kazak, Uzbek, Turkmen; by dying waters of the Aral Sea and oil-soiled Caspian Sea to the Caucasus Mountains of the empire strategic country of Georgia. Spanning the gap between the Caspian and Black Sea independent Georgia has long been a thorn in the foot of the Russian Bear. A land bridge between the Caspian region and Europe.

Mount Elbrus, Caucasus Mts.

A particular thorn in Russia's foot, Pankisi Gorge on 42.08 N latitude is one with an attitude. The refuge of Chechen and Islamic State terrorist fighters and training camps, Pankisi Gorge is a rip in the torn Georgian lands where the tug-of-war between Iran, NATO, and Russia ply for empire dominance and control over this strategic energy corridor of the Georgian Caucasus.

At its western end, the Caucasus mountains join the Pontic Alps of northern Turkey at the Black Sea. Another transverse range along the 42nd the Pontic Mountains is the upwards thrust of the Anatolian Fault of Turkey's north coast. Another mountain range of stunning beauty, this verdant dragon out of western Asia, blends the ying of Black Sea waters with the yang of Pontic Mountains into a conduit of earth energy to the "City of the World's Desires"—Istanbul.

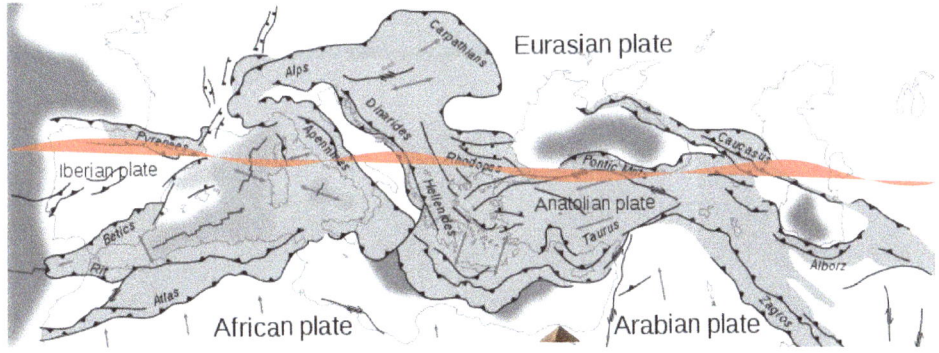

Byzantium, Constantinople, Istanbul is a bridge on the Bosporus strait between the Black and Marmara seas. Poised between East and West,

Asia and Europe, at the height of mountains and depth of the sea, this city of Constantine, happiness, and Islam, is desired for its strategic location, beauty, and wealth. Centered at the crossing of north, south, east, and west; the telluric power of fault line below and spires above, Istanbul is a coveted sacred site focused by the seven sacred directions of creation, the many domed Hagia Sophia.

More a religioscape than building, the Hagia Sophia, or Holy Wisdom, harkens to a time when this third aspect of the Christian Trinity was spoken of in the feminine tense. Completed by Emperor Justinian I it served as a bishop's seat and symbol of Imperial power and divine authority; he was quoted as saying "Solomon I have outdone thee".

Belying its status as world wonder and most beautiful building on earth, Hagia Sophia's history is one of war and religious schism. Played out in both material and spiritual realms, this iconic symbol and story embodies the polarity that is the 42nd deadly ley line. To speed its construction, building blocks and columns of once great Greek temples were placed as foundation stones for Hagia Sophia. Not unlike the state religion, Constantine created to unite his empire with the one faith of Christianity. Like the stone of Sophia divergent pagan groups were brought into line by including their myths and traditions as foundation stones in this faith drafted in testament as the Nicene Creed in 325 CE.

A city emblematic of Western power and religion in the Levant today, Istanbul and Hagia Sophia is an enduring reminder of Islam's triumph over the West and Christianity. Conquered by Mehmet II in 1453 CE, Constantinople became officially known as Istanbul in 1930 CE after being the jewel of an empire for 1600 years.

The seat of the Ottoman Caliphate and Empire Mehmet II fulfilled Prophet Muhammad's conquest hadith "Verily, you shall conquer Constantinople. What a wonderful army that army will be, and what a wonderful commander it will that be."

Considered an impregnable fortress of the era, Mehmet II used a brilliant war strategy with the loss of 20,000 combatants and 5,000 defenders to crush the Byzantine Empire and drive Christianity out of the Levant.

   A nodal point or standing stone on this 42nd bandwidth deadly ley the history of the conflict that is, Istanbul set a tone of conflict for the world. The one-time seat of 'the one true faith' of Christianity, it witnessed the schism between the Orthodox and Roman churches. In the hands of Islam, the schism between Sunni and Shia vie for the honor of having the one true faith in the eyes of God. This polarity sounded in the call to prayer and the ringing of the bell echoes across the time to: Cain and Abel, Ishmael and Isaac, Romulus and Remus, Sunni and Shia, Orthodox and Roman, North and South. This polarity inherent to the human condition has been used for the advancement of empire through war, both material and spiritual, and has motivated the violence of brother against brother until habituated along the deadly ley lines of the world.

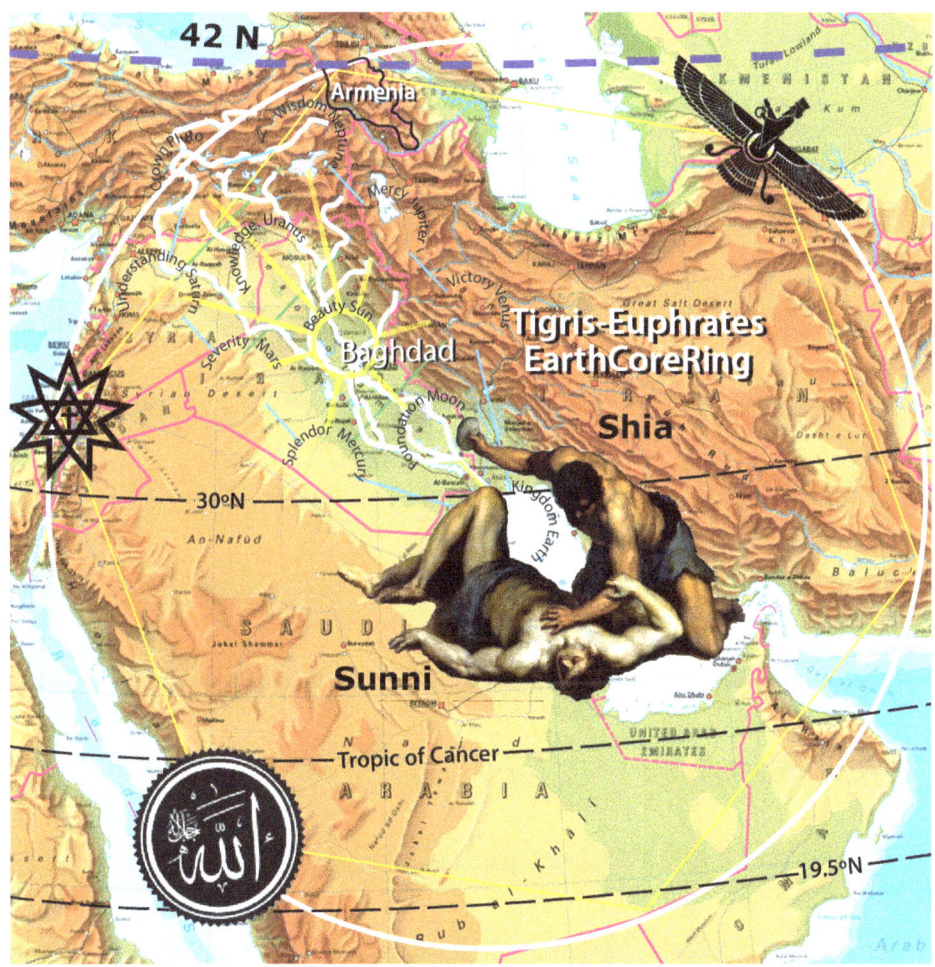

Spinning like a Turkish dervish we whirl, along the 42nd, in the sound wave of "Hu Allah", out of Rumi's Turkey and into the Balkans for more historic suffering along this ley.

Like Istanbul, the Balkans are a place between the Islamic and Christian worlds. A zone of friction that has inspired the violent cruelty of both Vlad the Impaler of Romania and Slobodan Milosevic of Serbia. Poised between the megalomaniac egos of empire, carried on this sound wave and deadly ley line through Europe, the Balkans have been bullied and have been heroic in response across this peninsula's trauma triangle. And so we begin our 470-mile (750K) journey from the Black to Adriatic seas.

Landing ashore in Bulgaria, we leave what was in pre-flood times a valley paradise now filled with a black sea, we follow the transverse Balkan Mountain Range through the center of Bulgaria from its coastal east to mountainous west where multiple blood-stained passes have witnessed battles for sovereignty, against successive invading empires who died in their quest to be number one. The ramparts of the Balkans, these mountains were as effective a barrier as any walled city to enemy siege. A neighbor of Turkey, Bulgaria has withstood their advances with song, dance, Shopska Salad (woncka carnata), and Madara Horseman.

No stranger to empire, the First Bulgarian Empire had a good run of it from 681-1018 before Byzantine Emperor Basil II awoke the Bulgars from that dream. They had a second go at empire from 1185-1396. Ruled by Mongol Khans, invaded by Goths and Huns, resisting Islamic and various Turkish empires, Bulgaria remained by playing the two sides of political regimes to maintain its middle-ground identity as a country. A goulash of ethnicity and religions from Slavic polytheistic paganism to Christianity, to the heresy of Bogomilism (a precursor to French Cathars also along the 42nd who were the victims of the Albigensian Crusade), the Bulgars defined their world as north and south of the Balkan Mountains.

Known for their at times despot rulers, such as Tito and Nicolae Ceaușescu, the Balkans have been subjected to empire's tyranny positioned as they are between: Rome and Greece, Holy Roman and Ottoman, Soviet and NATO. The birthplace of Alexander the Great (336–323 BCE) in Balkan Macedonia gives face to this nexus of empire along the fourity-second latitude. At the crossing of two deadly leys, the Balkans have historically been stuck in the trauma triangle focused by the crossing of the toxic patriarchal and empire leys found here.

Drawing the baseline of a 2 shape of the Balkan-Carpathian mountain chain, the Balkan Mountains rests upon the 42nd latitude as a symbol of a peninsula coming to terms with the polarity of life as "all is good" as put forth by both Bogomils and the White Brotherhood through Bulgarian mystic Peter Deunov; aka, Master Beinsa Douno (1864-1944). Deunov being a voice and force for an enlightened culture, sounded along 42nd throat chakra of the world.

At the junction of Balkan, Carpathian and Rila mountain ranges is Mount Rila and its sacred 'seven lakes' where Deunov's White Brotherhood gather every August 19th to perform a circle dance of paneurhythmy. With a thousand in attendance, their dance heralds and supports the eminent change of ages in a dynamic spiritual co-creative relationship with the Christ within, healing the memories of war over the past centuries..

Moving through the sonic wall of Bulgaria into the one-time Serbia Empire, Bulgarian open throats sing the glottals (mini yodels) and ikns (high-pitched dissonance) on the 42nd throat chakra line, offering mournful tones for Kosovo dead.

Here, now, we enter the heart of darkness along this deadly ley line, "Field of Blackbird" Kosovo Polje or Kosova for short. This is where the 1389 battle between Serbian Christians fought the Ottoman Empire to a stalemate, leaving a field of blackbirds to feed on its carrion banquet. With the Ottomans eventually winning the battle due to their greater numbers, it was widely held as the end of Ottoman advances in Christian Europe. Both army rulers, Sultan Murad I and Prince Lazar, were included in this imperial feast of chopped liver on this field of blackbirds. A one-time empire, Serbia to this day is in the shadow of its imperial miasma.

Of the 50,000 who fought in 1389 Kosovo, there were casualties in the tens of thousands. A number only exceeded in the Serbian genocide of Kosovo Muslims in the 1995 Bosnian War.

One of the 10,624 wars fought by mankind in the historic era, Kosovo at the armature of two deadly ley lines is of particular interest as empires collide. Hellenistic, Roman, Serbian, Bulgarian, Byzantine, and Ottoman imperial ambitions have set their similar but unique frequencies in the Earth that seemingly perpetuate the empire's pyramidal impulse.

A relic of its one-time greatness, Serbian memory of empire held the Kosovo minority responsible for Ottoman sins against its fatherland in their Bosnian genocide where 34,000 were killed and another 30,000 displaced. Such numbers give one pause. Why is such carnage and polarity focused along this parallel? Human nature? ET control? Is Satan having fun with free will? Certainly not the God that is Love, or as the Bogomils would say "It's all good", even the struggles and suffering of life, as the Bogomils believe that God created all, both good and evil.

Before leaving the Balkan Peninsula, while cooling off war heels in the Adriatic Sea, one last stop on our pilgrimage is warranted. Certainly, a spiritual agency of evil was present in the Bosnian War. Countering this force of evil, Our Lady of Medjugorje blesses hearts with the light of God's Grace, from Medjugorje's Apparition Hill. Communicating with six individuals relating 10 secrets she informs us, like Our Lady of Lourdes, also on this planetary wave, "I have come to tell the world God exists. He is the fullness of life, and to enjoy this fullness and peace, you must return to God."

Relaxing a little at the Cafe Imaginarium in the Harbor of Bar in Montenegro, we pause to reflect on the journey through empires of the Balkan. Enjoying a cup of Turkish Coffee makes one wonder what lasting legacy these empires left antecedents besides a good cup-a-joe. What is this impulse towards empire?

Playing god with divine authority, imperial might vanquish the 'other' while developing a world culture through invention with its drive towards dominion. Roads, universities, multiculturalism, spiritual development, and invention have all been byproducts of the human sacrifice that enabled empires. Few people have suffered as much as the Slavs of the Balkan Peninsula. And few have contributed more to the spiritual and intellectual development of mankind than: Deunov, Plato, Tesla, or

Medjugorje.

Surviving imperial will an epi-gene remains, trading places from survivor to victim to hero to bully as an impulse in Serbians and Bulgarians to once again know the greatness of the empire. Attempting to side-step this impulse a spirited observer Peter Deunov offers. "The Slavs will be united; they will be the bridge between Europe and Asia. All Slavic people need to unite into one. After the unification of the Slavs, the whole world will unite. The future people of Love will unite all. The Slavs will introduce a spiritual element into the world—that we may become as brothers. Their mission is the unification of all nations." This itself a statement of empire, albei spiritual in nature.

Looking west across the intoxicating blue of the Adriatic to the spur of Italy's boot and Rome, one wonders what benefits to life and love the Roman Empire(s) have gifted the world.

Disembarking onto the shores of the Testa del Gargano peninsula on Italy's east coast we offer: Ciao, Salve, Buongiorno, Buondi, salutations of the day to Saint Michael at Santuario di San Michele Arcangelo of Manfredonia; offering a tip of the halo from Medjugorje of the Balkans to all the saints of Apennine Peninsula. Likely well marked, as "all roads Lead to Rome" the journey of empire begins across the 200 miles of Italy's 42nd latitude.

Synonymous with empires, Rome gave the world its first Republic, interstate highway system, and a sports coliseum every few hundred miles, with promises of both "bread and circus" at the next exit. Known for its despot god-enabled Cesar or Mussolini of both ancient and recent holy Roman empires, its worldview marches on. As this passage is written, a social

media trend is being followed where women ask their men, "How often do you think of the Roman Empire". Their answer "often". The Roman Empire is perhaps held by males as an ideal to strive for, and is played out in rulership over parking spots or the construction of neo-baronial suburban mansions.

To be part of an empire is intoxicating. A vicarious experience of godhood in your 'hood'. To have free will is to be like gods, proven with each vanquished foe, be it mouse or man. A template that profits from the suffering of others, and requires redrawing if the world is to move beyond its glaring limitations.

A tempering phenomenon of the empire has been its holy men. Where would Jesus be now if not for Judas to betray and Rome to crucify? An imagined and real threat to the Empire of Judea, Rome helped Jesus Christ seed its empire with his testament to love into the hearts of humanity and the saints of Italy. Italy tips the scales for the most saints at 1077, 10% of the saints from around the world. Tempering and retraining the 42nd with an ecstatic love for Christ, man, and animal; we find the stones laid by the stigmatic hands of Saint Francis in Assisi on this same road to Rome.

Saint Frank used local limestone of the Apennines Range, as did Rome. The closest we can get to a living rock, its calcite was formed by layers of equatorial coral reef. Found around the world from Antarctica to Rome, it suggests from its geologic distribution that either the whole of the earth was equatorial during the Pleistocene Age, or the equator moved around a lot during that age. However this rock of civilization got there, limestone has been building blocks of culture because of its versatility and ease of quary. A sacred stone one could say, as it underlays the holy precincts of the Yucatan, Giza, Jerusalem, and Greece. The anthropomorphic bones and ganglia of the world and their attenuation to frequency transmit nerve signals of empire throughout its worldwide deposits.

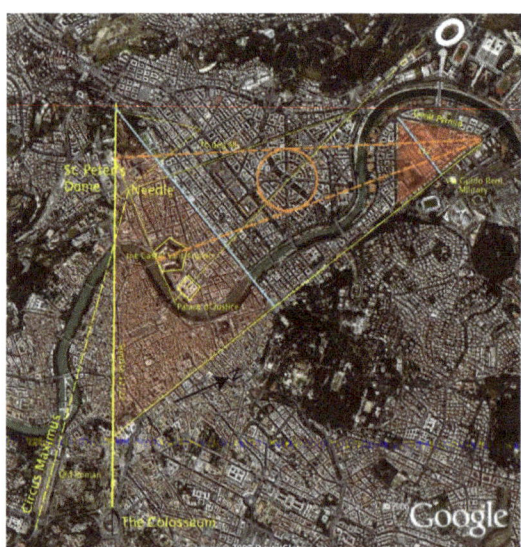

As one empire dies, the next empire use their foundations. The Holy Roman Empire overlaying Roman Empire in syncretism, making the old new, as Rome's geometric patterns attest. Just upstream from Rome along the river Aniene, the Roman travertine/ marble quarries of Tivoli were used to build and adorn Rome. First discovered in the 3rd century BCE, it is this 'stone from Tivoli' that Saint Peter's Basilica was made. The Romans used the same limestone to construct their aqueduct, allowing for the baths and hygiene enjoyed by slaves, senators, and Caesar alike. Assembled in the sacred geometry of nature's proportions, such cultures nested in the fabric of the world enjoyed empire runs of a thousand years.

A model to be replicated by succeeding emperors, Rome's empire stretched from Spain to Armenia setting its frequency of dominion into world consciousness. Approximately 3000 miles wide, the Roman Empire covered more than 1/5th of the 42nd latitude's 16,104 mile length. To once again apply correlative thinking, thought non-causative  by scientific thinking, the east to west breath of the Roman Empire, marked a pentagram's division on this latitude. Spinning at the speed of sound this empire proclaimed: "Roma Invicta, Gloria Exercitus, Senatus Populusque Romanus". (Unconquered Rome, glory to the army of its Senate and people.) Now that is one witch's spell upon the world, enlivened by the life supporting phi ratioed pentagonal framing of this latitude of empire.

Emulating the Roman model, there have been 50 to 70 empires historically. Much of what we call history was written in the blood of the empires. Hanging like Italian tomatoes of the 42nd vine, the largest empires of history does not include Rome. The top three empires are the British, Mongol, and Russian Empires; but Rome remains as the icon of empire in the collective imagination, largely due to its deadly use of crucifixion. The British thought of themselves as bringing civilization and order to the world. Many of the perpetual war-torn places around the world were once a part of the British Empire—upon which the sun never set.

The sacrifice of human life was not the only driver of the empire, the others being the horse and the tree. Felled by the millions, the trees of the world built ships, fortresses, and empires. They burned as fires and siege towers. The cedars of Lebanon are a memory left in the wastes of the Ottomans. I'm god, no I'm god, no I'm god—the divine mandate continues to pit Cain against Abel to this day.

After millennia of all manner of orgies, the weary travel stumbles down the seven hills of Rome to the delta of the Tiber River and the seaport of Ostia to hop a Corsica Island bound Navis Longa (Long Ship) on our way to the Pyrenees transverse mountains of the Iberian peninsula.

Dropping anchor in the bay of Ajaccio, we make our way ashore to fill our Roman-stretched stomachs with zuppa corsa at Tra Di Noi in sight of our ship dwarfed by the container ships of far-off tax havens. As it turns out, our host informs, that a small-statured fella with the fiery temper and cold hand, Napoleon Bonaparte (NB) was born here in Ajaccio on the 42nd parallel of latitude. Who knew?

Rising through the ranks during the French Revolution, Napoleon quickly replaced the guillotined royals as new sun king and emperor in 1804 at the age of 35, as Saturn squared his Sun. Seizing the day in ten short years Napoleon cannoned a small but fiery empire from the European landscape. Defeated at Waterloo and Russia, NB took on the Great Pyramid for crimes against humans, but lost to its silent stones returning home defeated with the cannon-shattered nose of The Sphinx on the good ship Muiron to the waiting smelly embrace of Josephine. Elba and Saint Helena bound the spirit of Napoleon granted, with imperial decree, passage to the Golfo de Roses where we are expected for dinner at Castello d'Empuries at Empuriabrava, Spain.

At the gateway of the Spanish Empire and Pyrenees, Emporion was a Greek and Roman colony. Emporos, or "one who travels", is at the crossroads of trade and the empire of Spanish of Castile. Coming to the end of our journey along this deadly ley line across Eurasia, it was from Spain that Italian Christopher Columbus sailed the ocean blue carrying the 'doctrine of discovery' and empire to the Americas. It is this bearer of Christ that leads the pilgrimage westward along Camino de Santiago.

Just north of the 42nd, the Pyrenees Mountain Range were the battlements of the empire for 700 years between the Christendom of the Holy Roman Empire and the Islamic Caliphate of Wilayat Al-Andalus. Spotted with Templar Knight commandery along their 600-mile length, this mountain range marked a divide between worldviews like other transverse ranges on this deadly ley.

A line of conflict into the 21st century, Basque and Catalan separatists have sought for independence from Spain in vain, in the rain on the plain. Bridging worlds of French and Spanish temperaments, nearby mountainous Principality of Andorra was created by King Charlemagne to keep Islamic Moors from advancing into Christian France through Andorra's mountain pass. Once used by Hannibal in the Punic Wars with Rome, Andorra is now a tax haven hosting the world on its ski slopes amid memories of the empire's dream.

In parallel with Medjugorie's 43.02 N is Lourdes on 43.07 N where another Lady of Light has attracted millions of prayerful pilgrims to its northern Pyrenees foothills and holy healing spring. Inspired by 18 visions of "the immaculate conception" in a grotto by the long-suffering

Saint Bernadette Soubirous. Afflicted with TB and asthma, at 35 years old, Soubirous suffocated like one crucified. Drawing the world faithful in prayer to its 'Sanctuary of Our Lady of Lourdes', its holy waters give healing to body and soul to those of faith, prayer, and penance.

Drinking from its holy water suffering is eased as an expectorant, disgorged from the grotto's gape, of empire's inhumanity, held as memory in body and soul, in this throat of the world. These apparitions of Lourdes and Medjugorje are strung as Rosary beads are worn as world necklaces, transforming fear into love along the 42nd.

Ever westward, the Pyrenees turn from border to coastal range at the Hendaye Cross in France, where the east coast of France meets the north coast of Spain. This cross is said to be a message for the ages to come marked in symbol, geometry, and place. It is at this transitioning geography and time that the symbol for the Camino de Santiago or Way of St James begins.

The Camino de Santiago is one of three main pilgrimage routes of Christianity, along with Jerusalem, and the Via Francigena to Rome. Made of several routes, the Camino's end goal is Santiago de Compostela, the designated burial site of Saint James the Apostle.

A path of penance since the 10th century CE, the Camino is lit by the Milky Way overhead, and called Voie Lactee in French. The pilgrimage leads to Cape Finisterre, the end of the world in Latin. The Camino was imagined as a path of starlight, whose Pyrenees Range's alignment pointed to Jerusalem. Seen as the stars of the Milky Way projected to

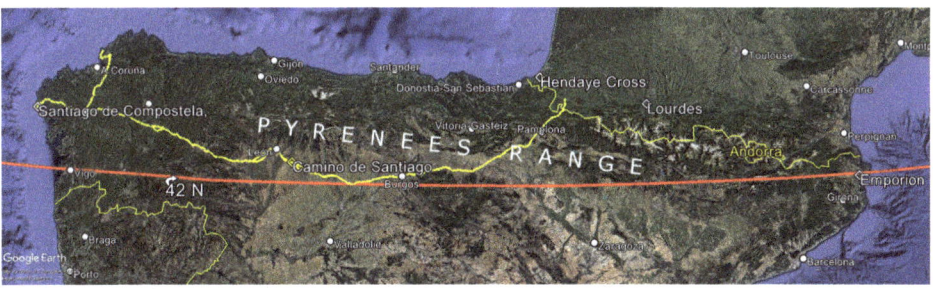

Earth, as a kind of Star Knowledge, its many churches and shrines were seen as their mirrored river of lights leading back to Jerusalem. Following the setting equinox sun, pilgrims were guided westward in dreams of empire across time and the Mediterranean Sea.

Traveling westward our pilgrimage books passage on the Mayflower. Making landfall in our next leg of our journey of empire around the world we step ashore in Plymouth, Massachusetts, New World, North America—1620.

While Christopher Columbus and Spain were the first imperial powers to make their mark on this "new world' (to them), it was the culture of New England's Pilgrims that grew as an empire into the United States of America.

Marked by Plymouth Rock, it was here on the 42nd where for 40 years Metacommet's severed head rotted on a pike at the gate to Plymoth Plantation. With this head of war sachem, King Philip's (Metacommet) War, an example was made and repeated in the 270-year genocide of Indian Peoples that followed. Arriving in a mostly empty land already ravaged by European disease, and with endless numbers of European empire's diaspora to follow, there was little hope for the continued sovereignty of its native peoples. In a ceaseless march of empire across a continent, Europeans did unto others what was done unto them in 500 years of Inquisition and millennia of war.

A line of scorched earth across the continent, our 42nd is drawn by state boundaries and more transverse mountain ranges. Marking a state boundary of nineteen states and one province, the 42nd road empire's impulse across the United States, Inc.

From Massachusetts' Great Falls massacre where brave Captain Holyoke skewered babies with a saber through Albany and Erie Canal to Buffalo, Detroit, Lansing, Chicago, and the 'breadbasket' of the American—empire's impulse laid waste sovereign first nations.

Westward on the 42nd, Bringham Young led Mormons to Utah's traverse Uinta Mountain range and established yet another brutal theocratic empire on the 42nd. Taking the Oregon Trail over South Pass (Wyoming) Continental Divide, Young was accompanied by thousands of empire's refugees, claiming Indian lands as empires of one.

East-West mountain ranges, thrown up with the sound of earthquakes from Mount Holyoke in Massachusetts to the Siskiyou Mountains on the California-Oregon border the 42nd, as in Europe and Asia, one finds a deadly ley line of nature and culture, from the Atlantic to Pacific and the Great Lakes between.

At the center of tectonic North America, Mount Holyoke is central to Ivy League universities transmiting the American populist version of empire along 42nd latitude. Supporting this populist empire from above, USAF; a Strategic Air Command ruled the skies from an underground bunker inside this mountain range until the 1970s.

Starting in earnest in the 17th century, colonialism became the empires of the day. Driven by a discorporate entity, the emperor and king took a subservient role to the world's disembodied corporations. Nowhere was this hidden ruler more instituted than in the Americas. And it was in the United States where the 42nd impulse towards empire burgeoned in bandwidth; "What is good for business is good for America."

With a greed never before experienced, a kind of hyper feudalism with a new kind of untaxed royalty, entwined in discorporated economic relationships, wealth was not based on heredity but on sociopathic narcissistic genius. With the same serf class in servitude the corporate pyramid subsumed the Egyptian model syncretically.

What was once overt human sacrifice of old, now became a sacrifice not for religion and kingdom, but in service to discorporated entities. Not too dissimilar to Baal/ Moloch or whatever mask the adversary Ahriman finds convenient and stylish for the time, the first born is still offered up in fires of war and abortion.

Controlling a subservient population presented the same problem for all empires. Controlling the indigenous population in the way of increased profits; profits were made, killing another bird with the same stone, with the introduction of addictive compounds in problematic populations. Native Americans got alcohol to rob them of sovereign spirit and land. The Chinese got opium. The African Americans got heroin and crack cocaine. The worthless eaters got fentanyl. And everyone got tobacco and addictive food additives, ensuring profits and controllable populations. This profit through suffering drove trans-Atlantic trade in a desperate triangle of slaves, rum and tobacco that made the fortunes for the hidden families who sell weapons of war to all as modern day emperors. Reclaiming the human spirit in sovereignty and sobriety may just be the greatest fear of and threat to corporate empire.

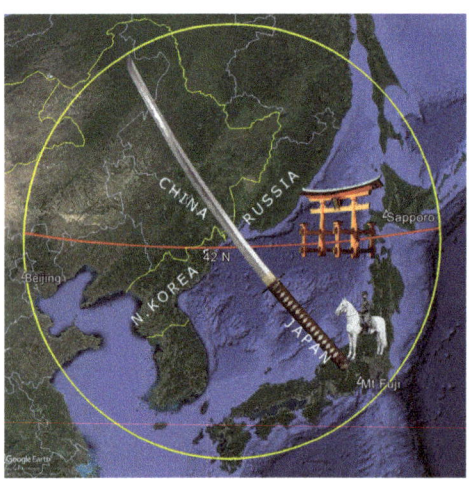

Completing this ring of trauma over the Pacific and back to Beijing, the 42nd ley cuts across Imperial Japan at the throat of its seahorse. Completing its circuit on Hokkaido Island (the northern sea circuit), we pass through its Torii Gate into the scarred emperial landscapes of the 42nd latitude.

Made holy by our conscious awareness a new string is strung, and a new circuit is connected by its revelation. So tuned and connected to a higher state of being a 'Song of Bernadette' is sung. Played on pearled frets of the instrument's neck a new song is played by the mother of the world by Hagia Sophia in Istanbul, the Rila Mountains of Bulgaria, Medugorje, and Lourdes as a chord progression to a higher frequency of being, freed of the habit of war.

First Nations Ley

Embarking on a new journey along yet another deadly ley line, we start where we ended on the 42nd Empire Ley in Boston Massachusetts. A great circle, the First Nations Ley runs nearly parallel with the 42nd across North America. The story of their dual passage is one of great sorrow and loss by first nations, and one of thriving abundance for the empire's uninvited guests. Arcing westward it is through the Great Lakes where this ley reaches its most northern point in its great circle, before arcing southwest through Hawaii, and Australia before turning north through south and western Africa, and inlining back to Boston, where we begin our pilgrimage through the sacred landscape of 'the people'.

In the 1670s, leading up to the King Philip War in Massachusetts Bay Colony, the god-fearing Pilgrims as a 'final solution' transported its native populations to Deer Island in Boston Harbor to starve and die from exposure. The victims were mostly women, children and elders, as able-bodied men were exploited as slaves.

Considered subhuman for their resistance to all knowing godly, Pilgrims thought it their right to establish the new Jerusalem in the Native cultivated wilds of the Americas. First Nation populations were plowed under, along with their now commodified sacred landscape. Parceled out by deed through drunken contractual agreement and blunderbuss, pilgrim encroachment of this  new world was marked out as fiefdoms with 120,000 miles of stone walls in New England.

 This native experience in the Massachusetts Bay Colony was typical for colonial expansion whose trajectory this deadly ley line follows worldwide. In North America, this violent expansion was collectively called 'The Indian Wars'. Starting in Massachusetts with King Philip's War and ending at the iconic Wounded Knee Massacre in Oglala in the now state of South Dakota, these wars of attrition

lasted from 1609-1890. It is estimated that 56 million indigenous people died in the Americas from plague, violence, and starvation throughout this history—a history that continues into the present day.

As we embark on this pilgrimage of remembrance, the first celebration of Thanksgiving is recalled as a victory celebration by the joint Colonial and Native strike force against the Pequots whose usury was long suffered by local first nations. With the aid of English weapons, the Pequot seat of power was burned to the ground along with its 700 inhabitants. This was the first Thanksgiving football game where the home team won. Eventually, our journey will take us on a 'great circle' of sacred and deadly sites through North America, Hawaii, Australia, south and west Africa, and back to the site of those Pilgrim hunger games.

Hungry for lands deprived them by the royalty of Europe, the colonists followed a network of trails westward worn deep by 10,000 years of human trade into the interior. One such "Mohawk Trail" follows the setting summer sun along the First Nations Ley, known today as Route 2/I-90.

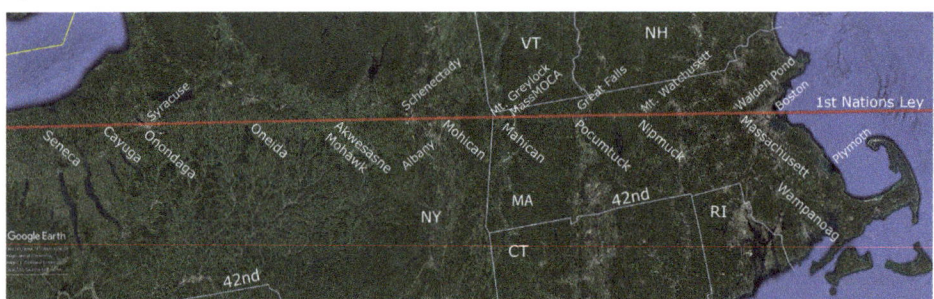

Marking its start at present-day Boston's City Hall Plaza, it was here where Bell invented the telephone and word was sent that "the British are coming" and Millerites experienced their 'great disappointment' that the world did not come to its end as predicted in 1844. Its long sorted history from native sachem council grounds, to red light district, to City Hall, it was the culture of Boston that won the west.

Ever westward, we stop for Transcendental reflections on the nature of nature with Henry David Thoreau at Walden Pond, in our beeline through Wachusett monadnock to the Great Falls on the Connecticut River of Turners Falls, Massachusetts.

Great Falls and other falls in the area were a community resource and shared by all the people up until the colonial land grab. A place of peace and spring gatherings for the annual fish run and mixing of the gene pool. A place of sanctuary for a day's travel, but if applied today would include the whole Earth. Sited in chapter on Empire Ley, Great Falls was a food resource for King Philip's War against the colonials. It was the Great Falls massacre of 300 women, children, and elders in the 1670s that the colony's call of "the only good Indian is a dead Indian", which was acted on with the greatest of zeal.

Traversing the Appalachian Mountain Range, our deadly ley follows the dead straight bore of the Hoosac train tunnel through the Berkshire hills connecting Boston to Albany, NY, Chicago, and beyond. Blasted with the first use of the explosive nitroglycerin, this 4.74-mile tunnel resulted in 196 deaths during its 24-year building effort in the late 1800s. Following the Deerfield "hardest working river", trains passed many water mills along its course that supplied weapon components to the Springfield Armory for the Civil War along this deadly ley. Exiting "The Bloody Pit" of the Hoosac Tunnel into the North Adams/Williamstown valley, the First Nations Ley crosses over Petersham Pass into the Mohican country of New York.

Following Route 2 through Massachusetts and New York states it is noteworthy that every form of Buddhism has retreat centers along this ley's course. Seen from Petersham Pass the chant of Nam ma Myoh ho Reng ge Kyo can be heard from the Peace Pagoda of Grafton as a supplication for world peace, answering the explosion of the  A-Bomb in the sect's native Japan. Changing Ley's deadly frequency, their chants serve to change the manifestation of its mass as a sonic wave form following its great circle.

Mitigating the memory of Christian-First Nations violence, carried as frequency by the First Nation Ley, the compassionate Buddha enchants the blue hills of New England. Drawing an axis, two Peace Pagoda straddle the Appalachian/Berkshires, marking the center point of this axis as a node on Ley. A stand of old growth White Pine trees were contemporaneously dedicated to native peace chiefs as 'The Trees of Peace' in Mohawk Trail State Forest. A conspiracy of Grace, these three places of peace were so named and built because of independent circumstances that allowed them to be. Constructed as a community effort the Peace Pagoda of Massachusetts and New York state were both gifted lands considered to be places of manitou by Algonquin peoples, so marked by stone spirit mounds in recognition of ancestors, place, or quest. The ring circumscribed by these three sites encircles the brain trust of the 5 college areas and all its spiritual and religious centers. The center of a matrix of landforms; the Coast of Maine, Connecticut River, Manhattan Island, and Jersey Coast all point to this center of North America's tectonic plate. Also aligning with this center of peace is the Mohawk River whose course is the most visible mark of the First Nations Ley in the land.

Rolling down the west slope of the Appalachian Mountains, spirit stones come to rest at the confluence of the Hudson and Mohawk Rivers at Peebles Island near Troy New York along the Mohawk Trail.

As we proceed deeper into Indian country an adjustment of terms is suggested. The name Indian is thought to be the result of mistaken identity by Columbus, who mistakenly thought he had reached India. The lands to the west of Europe were well known, much like the presence of aliens is known today but kept secret to maintain an illusory world view. Visited by seafaring Phoenician, Viking, and Carthaginian traders, these western lands were a source of bronze-age Great Lakes copper. Meeting the island peoples of the Caribbean, Columbus noted in this diary that they were a spiritual people, "in dios" or with God. Not following the scripting of what was to become 'The Doctrine of Discovery', the Spanish crown told Columbus to stop this nonsense and the name Indian was penned. Long despised the name Indian overlooked the diverse cultures of independent nations who lived in the Americas. In characteristic Native humor used to lessen the burden of the oppressive empire, the Indian Peoples have taken to calling themselves "NDN" in their collective identity outside tribal relationships.

Ndn of the Mohawk River valley called Mohawk were the tribe known as the Akwesasne. A misnomer assigned by French Canadian traders the Akwesasne were known to be cannibals or in their language mohawk. A deadly lot, the Akwesasne were feared near and far by all. Extracting tribute as a type of protection racket the Akwesasne guarded the eastern door of the Iroquois Confederacy by the promontories of Little and Big Nose at the river's bend in the village known as Canajoharie. Mirrors of their counterpart church inquisitors, the Mohawk were maligned as barbaric and deadly, and in need of conversion by Jesuit inquisitional missionaries. A node on the ley Our Lady of Martyrs Shrine was dedicated here for the tortured death of three Jesuit missionaries in 1640. Associated with this same shrine St. Kateri Tekakwitha (1656-1680) is exalted as the first Ndn saint canonized in 2012 for her 'white martyrdom' in total commitment to God in the face of nonlethal persecution.

A place of rich culture and history, the Mohawk River Valley and the Finger Lakes hanging from this ley have been a source of romantic literature, spiritual fervor, and political thought. Following the barges on the Erie Canal, we take in salt supply for the trek to Oregon in wagons made for this journey in Conestoga, New York. Securing our barge in present-day Syracuse, we make our way to the Onondaga central fire of the Iroquois Six Nation Confederacy, or in their word Haudenosaunee, for council with the elders.

Inspiration and template for the United States Constitution, Bill of Rights, and form of governance, the Haudenosaunee were guided by the "Great Law of Peace" that brought six warring tribes to peaceful coexistence by 'The Peacemaker'; whose true name is spoken only in ceremony. Both Jefferson and Franklin studied this social system from which they modeled their federal government with the glaring exclusion of the Council of Grandmothers, whose final rulings were made to benefit the seven generations that follow. In Ndn culture the men held council to debate the effectiveness of war, or other issues affecting the tribe and confederation, their conclusions were always brought to the grandmothers for final approval or ultimate rejection based on the consequences for the generations to follow.

In the Ndn world we, as human beings, are in a spiritual context to the seven sacred directions: North, South, East, West, Zenith, Nadir, and Heart center. Whether by Divine design or placement by geomancer George Washington, the birthplace of the Peacemaker on Bay of Quinte, Ontario, Onondaga Central Fire and Washington DC are all exactly at 77 W longitude. On a mark of time's fourth dimension, Onondaga is at DC's northern door of wisdom and DC to their southern door of growth and nurturance. Arising from the crossing of the 77th West and 44th North in the Bay of Quinte, these numbers of mastery in gematria herald the coming of a great soul who brought peace to a deadly ley.

To the victors go the spoils of war. Allying with the British in the American Revolution, Iroquois lands were targeted by General Clinton who scorched earth. Divided into 400 acre parcels as payment soldiers for their Revolutionary War service, this once great First Nation Confederacy became known as the "burned district". A sacred place imbued with prayers, ceremony, and centuries of peace, this scorched earth zone took on a new meaning when a spiritualist population was

attracted there. This Sedona of the day burned with the fire of spirit, inspiring abolitionist, suffragette, and utopian cults.

Crossing into the big sea shining waters of the Great Lakes, our deadly yet sacred ley enters into the largest body of freshwater on earth. Grave waters to 30,000 souls have made the lakes hollowed. The reader may recall one of the Great Pyramid's deadly leys coursed along the south shore of Lake Ontario. With Ndn country populated by Huron and Ojibwa 'Three Fire' confederacy, the lakes give a visual impression of a vortex spiraling into Sault Ste Marie, an Ojibwa burial ground. Passing through Mount Pleasant Chippewa Indian Reservation at the center of the Michigan 'mitten', the hand of Creator, witnessed the attempted dissolution of a now resurgent Ndn culture. It was in the manitou spirit of these Great Lakes that this book was written in Meridian Township, Michigan.

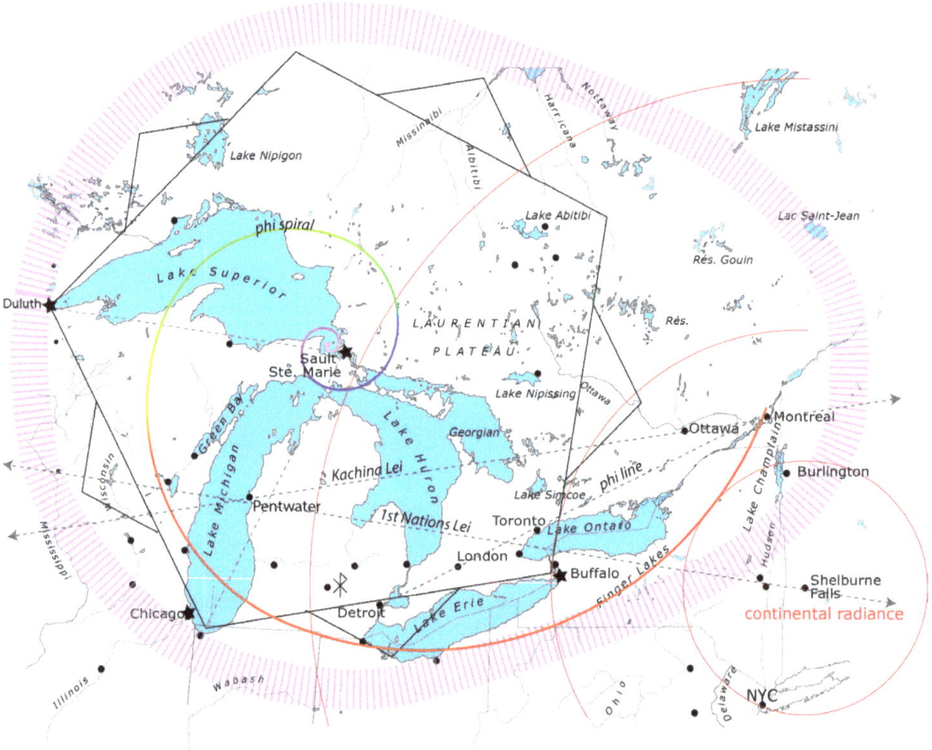

Portaging Wisconsin's unglaciated "Driftless Zone", Mississippi River, to plains we arrive at our next node of Pipestone on the Minnesota/ South Dakota border. The quarry source of calumet/ chanupa/ peace pipe stone, the place whose pipestone links all First Nations as people through prayer.

Quarried only from this place for more than 3000 years Pipestone's red metamorphic argilite was carved into a pipe bowl to which a wooden stem was affixed. Prayers for the dead and living were offered through its sacred smoke. As Black Elk once said: "When you pray with this pipe, you pray for and with everything". Sealing every broken treaty with the U.S. government authority, the iconic chanupa of the Lakota is a sacred bond and trust that can not be broken by ndn peoples to this day

Continuing our journey along the First Nations deadly ley we come to Wounded Knee. South Dakota. The following is an article written by the author and first published by, New Observations Magazine, Issue #142, Healing the Heartbeat of America, January 2023

OUR WOUNDED KNEE

December 29, 1890, Wound Knee Creek "the day the west was won".

The expressed purpose of this article is to offer spiritual science methods by which the dead of Wounded Knee, Cheyenne, Oglala, and the greater Sioux Nation; as well as Native Americans in total can return to the rainbow light of the seven sacred directions: locally, geographically within the Northern Plains, and Turtle Island in total.

King and Land are One

Like the wound in the thigh of the Grail Legend's Fisher King, Wounded Knee is an open wound that pains the soul of America's kings, and its Native People; bringing desolation to their lands as the king and the land are One. Even the name Wounded Knee speaks to the crippling of a beautiful, loved, and needed Race of Man.

This wound that never heals was first opened in Massachusetts, my home turf, during the King Philip's War pitting tribes east of the Hudson River against colonial blunderbuss. It was at the Great Falls massacre

where a similar cowardly action occurred against peaceable Indians, where the T. Roosevelt war cry of "the only good Indian is a dead Indian" was first acted on as justification for the genocide of a race prosecuted over the next 200 years from sea to shining sea, culminating at emblematic Wounded Knee where a people's heart-song was attempted to be silenced, and their sacred circle of life was buried under the weight of a pyramidal church and state.

Circle Verses Pyramid

A simple clash of worldviews between that of the pyramid and sacred circle where in the first, the god is on high outside one can not abide with the god within the heart of the sacred circle, the human heart, where Jesus bids us to look. A Lakota holy man once said to me, "I worship no man". This shook me, seeing how I've placed guru, prophet, and savior as filters between me and an authentic sovereign direct relationship with the Great Spirit, with God, with All That Is. This heretical idea was met with witch burnings and inquisitional torture in Europe and then the Americas. Wherever the sacred circle of life was buried by the pyramid of power devastation results, as was the case here in North America where its earth-keepers no longer offer the volume of prayers they once did at sacred sites leaving Mother Earth to wonder what happened and question, where is the love of the People she once knew?

EarthRings

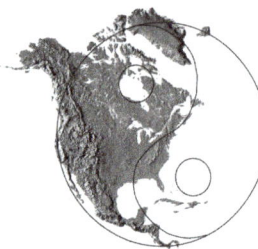

Like a cell, Earth is signaled and signals 'All That Is' through its bubbling biospheric membrane. The great Turtle Island continent is the diameter of Earth's core and Mars. It is one such bubble, whose pareidolian shape-form of a turtle has Mississippi lungs, Baja-Florida-Alaska-Maritime limbs, Canadian Shield head, and Central America tail was somehow known and spoken of in Native creation legends a shape that gives form to balance.

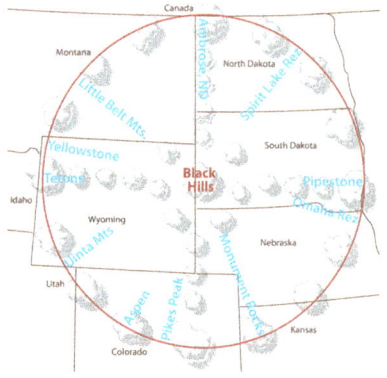

Like the 13 moon plates on the tortoise back, the great Earth Rings of New England, the Great Lakes, Northern Plains, Colorado Plateau, and the Sonora Desert are centered on granite sacred sites like Sapa Paha—the Black Hills. This greater turtle shell needs the light of man to keep its shell healthy. With the voice-dance of the Native nearly silenced by pyramidal power, the great turtle also suffers a wounded knee from lack of light, love, and joie de vivre that is emblematically caught up in the chain link fence surrounding the mass grave at Wounded Knee.

Their sin and offense, warranting murder of man, woman, and child, was the practice of the Ghost Dance, whose direct connection with the spirit world was a threat to the pyramidal power of both church and state. A kind of ritualized sacrifice, like that practiced by the Aztecs under the same pyramidal miasma, Wounded Knee, as the grand finale of the Great Sioux Wars, is emblematic of the intention of the day; "kill the Indian, save the man".

Masonic Suppression of Human Potential

Serving to suppress human potential, Native song has been toned down and silenced for too long. The sacred site, that Wounded Knee would have become, was co-opted in a syncretistic coup de grace by the conqueror the day, had the mass grave dug at a 33º NW angle sealing it as a pyramidal overlay. Not the first time the Masonic hand has placed their 33rd Degree seal over city and sacred sites as an American civilizing force the Church once fulfilled in my Grandmother's pagan Ireland. Control their sacred site, control its people. Being spiritually and emotionally co-opted, this sacred site formed a disconnect in the programming of the Native mind. The mass grave's 33°NW points to Rapid City, the antithesis of the ethos of Lakota spirituality. Its more culturally appropriate alignment would have been that of the Bighorn Medicine Wheel's 'sky burial' site, with its 23.5° ecliptic alignment towards starry home.

Furthering this agenda, the hand of Pte Oyate (Buffalo People) was likely guided by the whispers of Jesuit or Mason design to enclose the mass grave in a 77-foot concrete and steel berm, whose gate is held open by the iconic Masonic pillared portal of Boaz and Jachin. Done to appear more 'white' in the treatment of their Indian dead—it was done to gain the favor and respect of white controllers—but in effect suppressed the Native heart-mind under the weight of a pyramidal foreign culture

Numbered to resonate with the Washington Meridian of 77° West, whose syncretic overlay of the Iroquois (Haudenosaunee) central fire also on the 77th (whose federated democracy the USA copied)— Wound Knee grave site's dimensions numerically oscillate with the Washington Meridian's time tuned 77° W longitude. The mass grave's six-foot memorial obelisk (the size of a man), like the thousands of Egyptian Revival obelisks in the graveyard and city center; ground Washington's dominion over people and lands as antennas dialed to Washington Monument's 555-foot obelisk topped with its 55-foot pyramidion point.

Latitude with Attitude

Victims of history and circumstance, the Great Sioux Nations like many other civilizations worldwide who flourished between the 40th and 45th degree latitude, are in a Goldilocks zone on our Goldilocks planet. It is along these latitudes we find the clash of great civilizations occurred, from Rome to Constantinople (Istanbul), Genghis Khan, Beijing, and the Great Sioux Nation.

Wounded Knee's Pine Ridge Indian Reservation is central to a mythic landscape of star knowledge, a trauma triangle, as well as being the closest Indian reservation to Paha Sapa (Black Hills), or the 'Heart of All

That Is', and Mato Paha (Bear Butte), or "The Center of All That Is"

A kind of akashic library, Mato Paha is a pilgrimage and vision quest site for all the Northern Plains peoples—like a Mecca or Jerusalem of the Plains. A great attractor, Bear Butte draws 800,000 motorcycle enthusiasts yearly to Sturgis, SD in a pilgrimage upon spinning sacred circles dressed as leather-fringed memories of Native Americans to this place of spiritual power at nearby Bear Butte.

There is an ancient Hermetic adage; "change the frequency, change the manifestation of the mass". Oriented just 3 degrees northeast of the mass grave's 33º, its 30º realignment to Mato Paha would change its frequency to a 12 (360/30=12), orienting the mass grave site to the seven sacred directions, changing the frequency of masonic pyramid mind, to that of circle consciousness, freeing ghosted dancers from the dusty ruins of a long dead pyramidal culture.

Trauma Triangle

Bear Butte (Rescuer) rests in its mythic landscape after being mortally wounded in a great battle with a people (Victim) devouring monster (Persecutor) seen as the BadLands, whose dinosaur bones give testament to these mythic events. A trauma triangle with Victim (Pte Oyate) Persecutor (BadLands monster Unktehila) and Rescuer (Mato Paha) already in place since time immemorial, Wounded Knee was played like a cosmo-drama by the 7th Calvary Regiment (there's that 7 again) and the FBI who rode out of the BadLands to devour Spotted Elk's Band and Leonard Peltier.

With Rapid City set as rescuers through Wounded Knee's mass grave alignment, the ghosted dancers and lost Native souls are directed to Rapid City, rather than to return to the 'Center of All that Is', and the rescue of the Great Bear (Bear Butte, Mato Paha).

As if punctuating this misdirected 33º NW angle towards not so 'happy hunting grounds' sits the Grand Gateway Hotel—its exact alignment in Rapid City. In 2022 it instituted a ban on all Indians, despite being a hotel located on Black Hills treaty lands. Changing the frequency from this 33ºNW devouring angle of Unktehila to the grateful sacrifice of Mato Paha at 30ºNW would change the manifestation of this mass as expressed through such apartheid policies.

Ghosting the Dancers

My motivation and hope for service in writing this are to redress this ever-present wounded knee in 1st Nation collective consciousness. A consensus exists among those who sense such things that many of the Ghost Dancers were ghosted by a convergence of intentions, actions, and circumstances of persecutor and victim alike.

Encircling Spotted Elk's band, the 7th Cavalry formed an anti-life circle whose implosion of lead held intentions to ghost 'ghosts dancers', and cripple Indian Peoples with a wounded knee once-and-for-all. Further sealing the fate of these entrapped souls, survivors intentionally staked

victims with flags to earth where they fell, creating an emotion of ghosts in the new year's wind. Those with the 6th sense for such things say spirits remain attached to a highway cross placed as a memorial, by setting an emotional lock for both victim and survivor at its place of death.

Sealing this ghosted matrix of history and metaphysics of the mass graves, the 7th's circle of death cursed the Circle of Life with Hotchkiss machine guns spitting death upon souls with the priest's 'sign of the cross'; and then dumping dead knee to wounded knee in a masonic container, holding both dead and survivors in limbo, burying an Indian way of life. Now stuck, Spotted Elk's band of ghosted souls live through lost souls wandering the paths of Pine Ridge, Rapid City, and the greater Sioux Nation. It is now up to us all to dream of the return of our wounded knee's soul-shard from the spirit's shadow to the light of the Great Spirit.

Genocide of a People

Emblematic of the struggle of all Native Americans, Wounded Knee is also their sacred site as it was a seal of control over the collective heart of all Indian peoples. And, to this author's mind, it needs to be honored as a sacred site in a 1st Nation way. Not to imply that Wounded Knee has not been honored. Given the responsibility of Wounded Knee, the Oglala Lakota bore the burden given them by a convergence of circumstances. It is here where that massacre's echoing manifestations can be redressed.

In the land of the Blue Hills Peoples (Massachusetts), honor mounds of stone were placed in memoriam to events and sachem of note. Buried with desecration or not buried at all in the deadly contagion that swept away entire 1st Nation tribes, Wounded Knee could serve as a frequency to transform this mass of humanity as a remembrance place for the

Native holocaust. Perhaps with head-sized stones placed as Medicine Wheel by the all the tribes of Turtle Island whose sacrifice of lives and lands gave world peoples space to come together on common ground for common good. Celebrating this gift to the world in forgiveness and gratitude is one potential resolution to the victim cycle holding human potential and sacred sites in check.

She Who Watches

In the 40º- 45º North latitudes, 'She Who Watches' brought teachings to the world in Washington State, at Fatima, Lourdes, Medjugorje, and Mato Tipila (Bear's Lodge, aka 'Devil's Tower') where the White Buffalo Calf Women taught the people their 7 rites of moral life, as did the 'Lady of Light' in Fatima and Lourdes in their way. This lady of light, this White Buffalo Calf Woman, ('She Who Watches)', rides a red lightning bolt to renew and enliven that Native spirit, whose heart song is so missed by the Great Mother. Crazy Horse stands ready with hollow, hallowed bone-loaded travois to return them to the crackling summit of Mato Paha. There are mighty forces ready to aid the bold action of spiritual warriors by those who live the ways of the Chanupa as carriers of the White Buffalo Calf Woman's Pipe of Peace, sequestered from needful people and light of 'She Who Watches'.

Healing Collective Trauma

Changing the frequency of entropy so evident at Wounded Knee would usher Pine Ridge Reservation into a coherent reemergence of freedom that saves victim, persecutor, and rescuer from their repeated role plays so entwined in Wounded Knee's chain link fence and Leonard's cell. So freed the spiritual power that is Paha Sapa, waters the tree of peace at 'The Heart of All That Is'. Set by a sacred circle whose diameter lines between Grand Teton, Black Hills center Pe Sla and Pipestone, Minnesota, and walked by White Buffalo Calf Woman to Bear's Lodge, this turtle plate, this EarthRing of Turtle Island gives form, meaning, and spiritual power to Lakota cosmology. Based in context to America's Moon sized Mississippi arc of sacred site centered turtle plates for Native consciousness to once again maintain the world through spiritual warrior-ship.

Fat Eater with a Dream

The question remains though, who is this Wasi'chu (fat eater, white man), and who gave him the authority to write about such sensitive Native experiences? While an 'Indian lover', my experience can never fully appreciate the sacrifice that has been the Indian experience over these last 500 years.

I've come to this perspective in several ways. First, when I was seven years of age I had the same dream seven times of an elder on a mountain with a standing rock ring from which I flew over ever receding blue hills. These dreams set me on a quest for meaning. Chasing this dream through megalithic European culture and the general use of stone as a cultural medium, including 25 years of hard labor as a stone mason, led to the question: does the landscape express itself in geometric form like the rest of nature? The answer was yes and more, resulting in a body of work I call EarthRings.

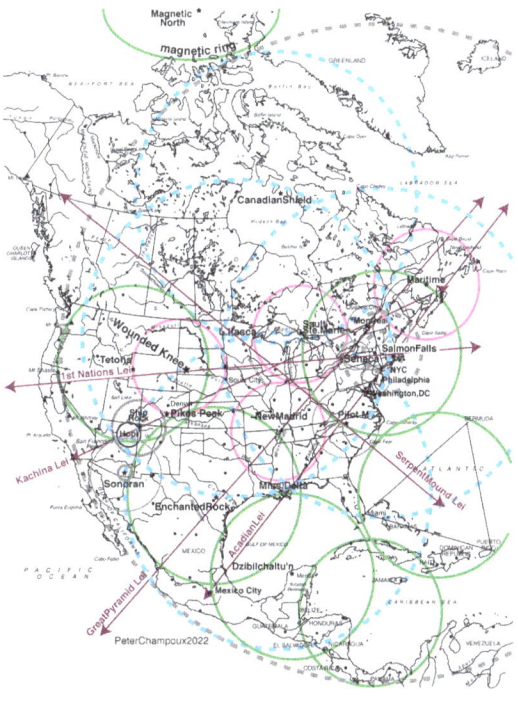

Contemplating this world view one can only conclude the Earth is a sacred place, a temple-like spaceship in the lighted waters of the galaxy. Developing this world view of the Earth as temple space my initial discovery was of geometry in the New England and New York landscape that brought Native and Colonial culture, mountains, and rivers, into a coherent "Gaia Matrix' whose alignments all pointed to Salmon Falls in Western Massachusetts, held by Native and Colonial treaty as a place of peace for a day of travel for fishery resource access. It was later discovered to be the center point of the North American tectonic plate—itself the only circular tectonic plate in the Earth's membrane. Manhattan Island, the Mohawk River, the Appalachian Mountains, and the eastern coastlines all point to this Salmon Falls center of a continent.

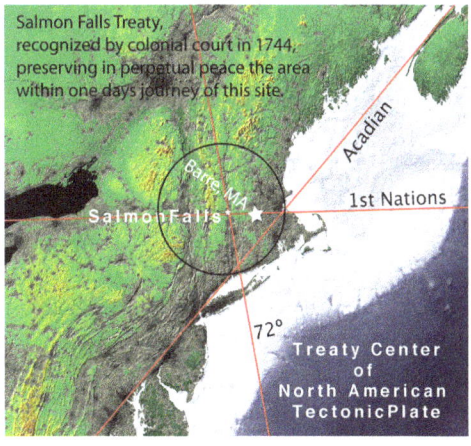

The baseline of this 'sacred geometry' of nature was the ancient pathway to the sea from Gitchigumi (Great Lakes) along New York's and Massachusetts' Mohawk Trail. Following this path westward along contemporary Route 2 from Boston in a straight line through Salmon Falls, along Mohawk River, and through the central fire of the Haudenosaunee Confederacy leads to Wounded Knee.

1st Nations Ley

Solidifying the alpha-omega Indian Wars dynamic between the Blue Hills and the Black Hills, Wounded Knee's looted ceremonial objects once held in Barre, Massachusetts form a line of Native genocide from continent center to Wounded Knee. The 'returning' of these Ancestors from Barre to Wounded Knee helps heal the memories of trauma held by this line.

An alignment entrained by the clash of civilizations along Goldilocks latitudes, this 'ley line', giving homage to Hawaii's Pele, is a great circle connecting indigenous culture through: Turtle Island, Hawaii, Australia, Zulu lands, and Yoruba of West Africa's slave coast. Memories can get stuck and repeated along such lei lines. One such virus in its software is Wounded Knee. I have found healing the blood memories of place returns such earth meridians to more balanced expressions of life ways. As an earth-keeper, I felt it my responsibility, given this knowledge, to write this report in support of Pine Ridge's work of the ages.

Maintaining the World

Like 1st Nation Australians whose didgeridoo, dance, and voices sing both earth core and song-line at sacred sites to maintain the world and connect with ancestors; 1st Nations Americans provide the same service with dance, voice, and drum at their sacred sites. Resonating to the sonic geometry of Earth's gravity field and the rest of creation, their sounding stimulates the vitality of nature maintaining the world. A service that needs support as a profession.

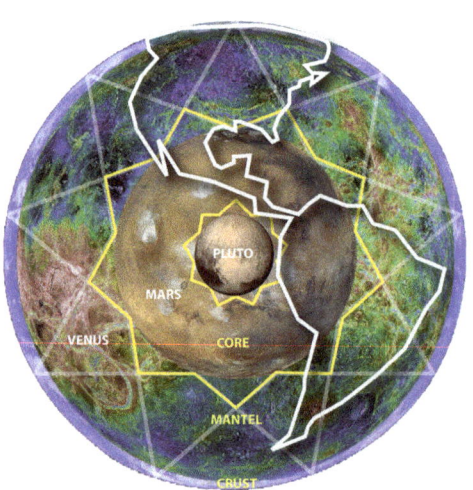

Ho'oponopono

So, I hope that through the awareness and release of these stuck emotions we might support our planet's emergence into a prophesied new era in the right relationship. Freed of the burdensome weight of the pyramid-mind, the sovereign 1st Nation heart-mind would be free to teach the world how to live in the right relationship with each other and our common ground—the Earth—our home. The king and the land are one. Accepting and acting upon this responsibility of spiritual warrior ripples as an intentional blessing across the Great Plains, Turtle Island, planet, solar system, and galaxy; heralding our inclusion into the greater community of Star Nations attending this awakening. Through our harmonized consciousness we make contact, heart-to-heart, as strong-kneed Ghost Dancers across the Milky Way. I'm Sorry—Please Forgive Me—Thank You—I Love You, …*

*this marks the end of the New Observations (#142) article on Wounded Knee.

Completing the First Nations path through continental North America, we pause for "rendezvous" in the shadow of the Grand Teton mountains. Called 'Grandmothers Who Stand Tall', these mountains stand as silent witnesses to the Yellowstone super-volcano whose potential eruption would be a deadly event at a scale never experienced by modern humanity. Aligning the Black Hills and Mount Shasta with the Grand Tetons on the First Nations Ley, these three mountains are all known to have a sacred relationship between humans and the spiritual world. Standing tall as Redwoods on the California coast, indomitable indigenous spirits of the First Nations book passage on HMS Resolution to Hawaii, the next node along deadly ley.

Not the best decision made by Captain Cook, of HMS Resolution, when on February 14th, 1779, did not find the love of Hawaian maid, found death along the First Nations Ley at the hands of Hawaiians, freeing of their ali'l nul (leader) Cook tried to kidnap for ransom. Hawaii is a vertical place formed by the volcano goddess Pele from the primordial ocean. Located on a planetary hotspot on 19.5 north latitude, this Hawaiian latitude is the same as the Sun's sunspot rings and the position of the largest volcano in the solar system on Mars. A latitude with an attitude, the 19.5 is on the nested baseline

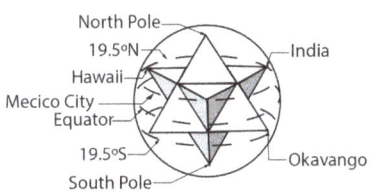

of a star tetrahedron 'merkaba' common to the sun and planets. This hot spot with a lens of water north-south-east-west focuses lava dome nadir through the volcano top telescope of Hawaii's starry zenith to the sacred island center in a confluence of earth-water-fire-air-ether.

Isolated, the first national archipelago of Hawaii lost 100,000 original people who gave it up to European disease. The denationalization of Hawaii followed with loss of culture and lands to the United States. Considered genocide by international law, its original People were reluctant to host an uninvited world to paradise.

The fiery eye of the world, with a view to stars, the First Nations' node of Hawaii informs earth-cell (Gaia); membrane consciousness, core, solar/ galactic current; and spiritual worlds super-sensibly of an experience of itself. Spiritual work here serves geophysical health. Neglected or forgotten by originals, sacred sites of old lady Gaia's geophysical spiritual health suffers from lack of good feelings in a ceremony that only humanity can bring. Aware of earth's elemental beings, Originals co-participated in planet stathis with footfalls, prayer song, and circle dance of intention; mirrors the world as alive in sacred space and place.

A 'Pearl' of a place, death came for 2,403 that December 7th day, and was followed by 15 million military and 38 million civilians over the course of WWII—may they rest in peace. Booking passage on ghost-ship USS Arizona, we sail WSW to Australia. A voyage of 20 days past Styx, we sail 4,958 nautical miles into Dreamtime.

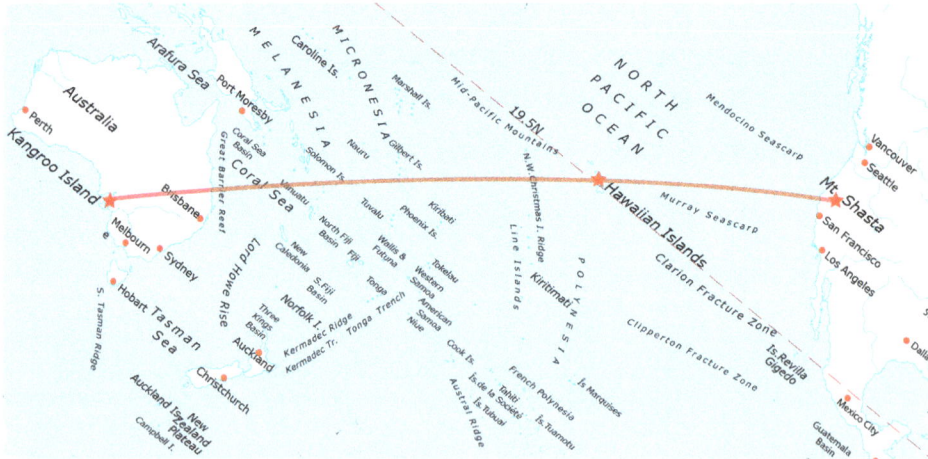

Genius has propelled civilization with invention, mostly with ever-greater means of mutual destruction. This gift of genius, unfortunately, is mostly specialized but tends to instill a superior sense of genius in all things, including those things genius knows nothing about. This narcissistic arrogance of Europeans at the expense of world tribes, who appeared primitive to their material genius, justified deadly consequences when worldviews collide.

In pre-colonial years, indigenous populations had their own highly developed genius unrecognizable to European conquerors. In 1491, the entire continent of North and South America was a highly domesticated sylvan culture where grasslands and forest were stewarded to benefit and maintain a balanced environmental system. Blind to Ndn genius, the colonials thought the abundance of the Americas was providential, not the work of a highly advanced, environmentally sound civilization that provided for all its native populations.

Every race and every person possesses a genius often overlooked by the 'other'. Perhaps condemned as racist, but it would seem every race has gifts others don't; who when brought into relationship, and recognized and applied, benefits all. So different are racial humans, their origins appear from different extraterrestrial peoples all born to Earth to work out the differences that divided their planet's peoples in perpetual conflict. 'Might is right' was entrained in the empire's minds that saw the destruction of cultures that could have provided the missing genius necessary to overcome the global issues confronting present-day peoples and places.

Sadly, it's generally true that where the English went trouble soon followed. A great sin upon the world, their legacy has been disproportionately borne by First Nations peoples across the United States, Australia, and southern and western Africa along this deadly ley.

Arriving at the dying Great Barrier Reef one enters the Dreamtime of Australia. The unknown southern land, terra australis incognita, Australia was inhabited by an unknown genius to the English colonials and convicts who invaded, and claimed in the name of Queen, the lands of the 'black fella'. The effete English, at a loss of fox for a golly hunt, hunted Australian peoples with guns, dogs, and horses for entertainment.

Every nation, mob, and clan of Australia's first peoples had distinct language, custom, ceremony, creation stories, and territory, but all were united in Dreamtime and Song Line.

Dreamtime is a worldview and way of being, seen in artistic expression, known in cognitive understanding, and seen in sacred landscapes. They are only now being understood within the scientific framework of developing quantum physics. Dreamtime has no time, no Past, Present, or Future. It is not a 'Be Here Now' in every constant moment in time, but more like a 'this', having all occurred simultaneously. Bridge to spiritual and material worlds, Dreamtime is an intimate co-creation with all that is. Or are the worlds of the Lokata, Mitakuye Oyasin... All My Relations.

First Nations Ley crosses Australia from Great Barrier Reef, through the Murray River drainage to vortexing waters of Spencer Gulf and Kangaroo Island, beyond and before, oscillating the quantum field with messages of absent ceremony at a world maintaining sacred sites and death of its world loving indigenous people. What a great loss to the world was the life and Aboriginal knowledge at the hands of materialistic Christian European colonials!

Called red devils and black devils, native peoples were considered expendable as part of Satan's work. And the world, considered evil in the Christian worldview, was thus exploitable. Evil, a byproduct of free will, is the realm of Satan. "Thy will be done on Earth as it is in Heaven", asks human beings to choose love, in free will, with all that is.

Sailing whale hunting waters of the southern Indian Ocean, we reach the farthest south point of First Nations Ley. Turning Northwest towards South Africa we arrive in Durban. Transecting South Africa, Botswana, Namibia, and Angola, our ley here has experienced its fair share of death at the hands of Zulu, English, and Pretorian apartheid.

Hopping the Gulf of Guinea, the ley grazes the slave coast making landfall in Liberia where Black ex-slaves were banished by a vanquished

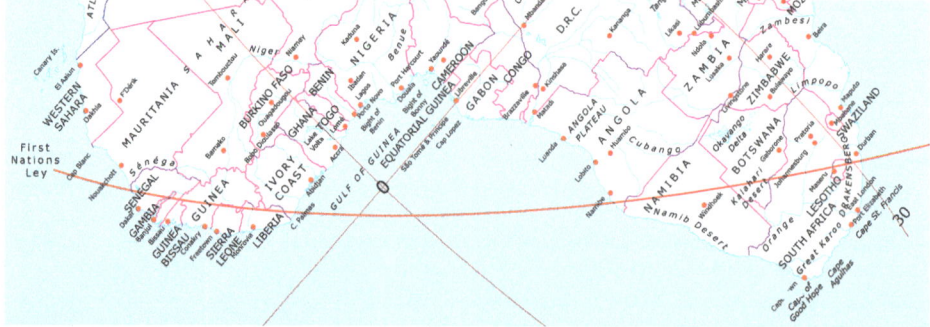

southern confederacy of the United States. Closest to the Americas, the enslaved departed from this coast to their "southern passage" oceanic graves. Carved up into colonial plots the nations and tribes of Africa have struggled for sovereignty in the face of European, Islamic, and warlord's misqualified use of will over Africa's Yoruba people.

Africa's Yoruban reluctant emissaries to the world conclave, hosted by similarly reluctant Native Americans, brought along with them a defining culture to the Americas.

Following the summer solstice sunset by Cape Verde Islands and over the tectonic Mid-Atlantic Rift, we complete our great circle of the First Nations Ley. Returning to Boston, landfall is made in the Yoruba-American Roxbury neighborhood of Boston. Settled on the geologic remnant of the once-connected continents, Roxbury was built on 'puddingstone' native to Africa, connecting First Nations Ley culturally and geologically.

A gift to the world put down by the blind genius of White European sense of superiority, First Nation peoples are at long last being recognized for their contribution to the human family as their worldview comes to the fore out of necessity. At the precipice of environmental collapse at the hands of the world's materialists, the earth's maintaining spiritual relationship with nature and its quantum field interface is a hope for the future. Putting aside the domination of white narcissistic materialists a greater spiritual context is discovered. That said name calling is not a solution, but the recognition of First Nations as equal is needed to become true stewards of Creation's gift, Earth.

Lessons learned as humanity and Earth now enter into a galactic context with "contact". Confronted with the genius of a million-year-old civilization, the roles are reversed. However seemingly superior to any people of Earth or Trithamador, we are in a quantum context with "All that is", in the First Nations world view. Learning from our mistakes, an open mind needs cultivation to accommodate the unknown contribution to world civilization and culture by: Forest People, Bigfoot, Sasquatch, Yeti, and Yowie.

The recognition of this ley, in itself, affects the quantum condition of the world timelessly. Giving intentional support to the world and maintaining ceremonies of the First Nation supports a quantum field that holds the world in health. "So the last shall be first, and the first last: for many are called but few chosen." Connecting the material and spiritual as one with ancestors in spiritual knowledge, humanity becomes co-creators with joy for all in its contemplation.

Returning to Boston Harbor, at the crossing of two deadly ley lines, we come to our last alignment

in this series. Stopping in for a Tea Party, at the dock of the bay, with colonial cross dressing as Mohawk warriors, we await the arrival of the British for "the shot heard round the world" in nearby Concord. Departing the First Nations Ley, we remember revolutionary Crispus Attucks, an African freeman, who was the first to die in the American Revolutionary experience at the Boston Massacre.

Awareness of this ley connects and reawakenens the Earth's original mind. Like the DOS programing always running in the background of Windows 11, the 1st Nations hold the original memories. The attempted suppression of 1st Nation sovereignty by the deadly colonial era has failed. This original operating system when rebooted overwrites western primed time based operating systems with aboriginal quanta based timeless OS.

PATRIARCHY in POLARITY

Acadia Ley

So named for the French Acadians who, in diaspora, were driven from their Nova Scotia home by the British, to the swamps of the then French-controlled Mississippi River Delta, where they "let the good times roll" to this day. A deadly ley that courses from Mexico to the Middle East, this ley's description in itself marks this

world as a planet of sorrows. Divided by the North Atlantic Ocean, its continuation through Europe and the Levant is a proverbial 'line in the sand'.

Plunging his obsidian knife deep into the chest of yet another sacrifice, the blood-soaked, exhausted, Aztec priest called upon Xochipilli, Kukulkan, and pantheon for the three hundredth time that day. With a few thousand eager victims to go, the Pyramid of the Sun was already slick with blood in the holy city of Teotihuacan at the Central American end of the Acadia Ley.

A frequency set, blood's perverted good answers Baal's call from past centuries at the other end of this deadly ley in the Levant 9,000 miles away.

Leaving the land of the living, Aztec victims followed the Avenue of the Dead 23.5 degrees northeast. Along the ecliptic of the solar system they would have traveled to revered Venus. Giving life as a force to the adversary Ahriman its anti-Christ intentions for the Earth was grounded with each knife thrust into this volcanic hot spot on the 19.5 N latitude. Grounding anti-life into planet Merkaba, the thousands sacrificed at Teotihuacan set a tone of discord on the Acadia for world wars that would have destroyed humanity if not for Christ overcoming his own sacrificial death.

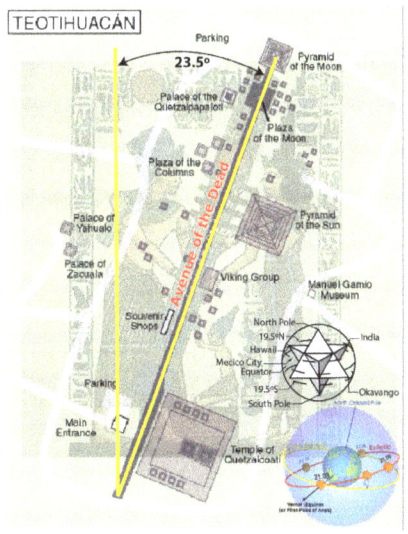

Healing the trauma of those along death's avenue, with a cascade of roses from Guadalupe's image, the survivors of Spanish Inquisition and Mixica blood sacrifice saw in its miraculous image a vision of a compassionate future. Having fully repopulated all those lost, we leave the 21 million souls of Greater Mexico City to siesta or fiesta in their palace of roses.

Leaving Teotihuacan through abundant Veracruz (True Cross), we ride the whirlwind across deadly hurricane spun waters of the Gulf of Mexico. Making landfall in hypoxic waters of the Mississippi delta's 'Gulf Dead Zone', we slog our way through its deadly waters to New Orleans.

Letting the good times roll, the Cajun Creole, like so many of the world's oppressed, are quirk to find joy in life's irony. Fresh off the boat from famine's predations, Ireland's sons died as chattel while digging by hand the gator-snake-mosquito-infested channels of New Orleans. Deemed too risky for valued slaves, the "hard to kill" Irish laughed in the face of death, developed over centuries of interactions with Viking and English overlords. A mardi gras of world culture, the drums of its Congo Square gave rise to the American cultural experience in its mix of continental waters caught in the petrochemical eddy of New Orleans.

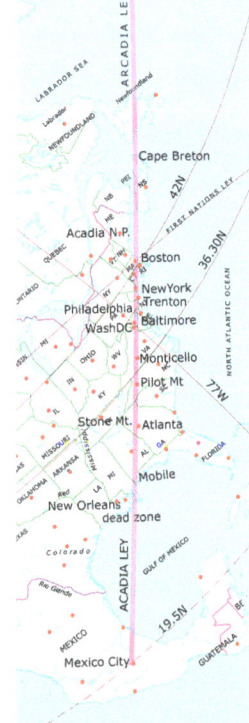

Root of both Mississippi River and Acadia Ley, the French bookend its passage through the aligned megalopolis of the east coast of the United States. In a beeline through Mobile and Montgomery, Alabama, by orchards of "strange fruit", and Martin's dream, the South knows the wrath of master and oppressor in Sherman's March to the sea after burning Atlantan rebels in a fever of retribution. This classic example of a deadly ley line is a string tuned tight by the economies of suffering. From New Orleans to Nova Scotia, through Atlanta, Monticello, Washington DC, Baltimore, Philadelphia, Trenton, New York, New Haven, and Boston a crow would be hard-pressed to find a straighter line of culture and nature and predation.

Native genocide and relocation, prosperity through slavery and tobacco addiction, and profiteering from near endless war throughout its colonial and republic period, its designation as a deadly ley line is well earned.

What we explore are the reasons why such good

people full of love, are in the company of comedian Bill Murray, caught in an ever-repeating 'Groundhog's Day' of war. A habit formed in an empire but introduced in a cave, profit through suffering and service to self has been a path of least resistance followed by the cannibal royals of the military-medical-insurance-banking-political-industrial complex since forever, whose wake failed to raise all boats.

Arguably, alignments of war could be found in any direction on our war-ravaged planet. What we seek to unlock are the shackles that bind humanity, like Scrooge and Joseph Morley, freeing our compassion and humanity.

Dividing the circular North American continent in two the Acadia Leys entrains its Mars and Earth Core diameter plate with a message of war to the world. A continent of half land and half water, its balanced shape in metaphor could bring harmony to the world as a power of place.

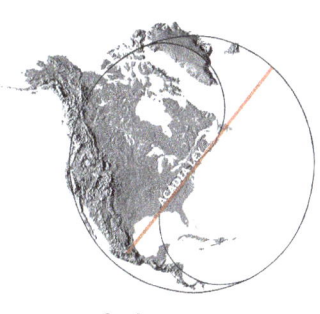

With turbos screaming, patriots plow through rice grinders in F-16 Dominator, with AR-15 gun rack ready for next school yard, at 20 MPH over the speed limit northeast on I-95. All the while speeding past city center after city center war memorials, affirming America's greatness and sorrows. In a skunk cloud of smoke, America kicks back with opioid-laced, endocrine-disrupting pizza, to enjoy the bread and circus of once flayed Washington Redskins. Returning to castle-keep, America's warrior class settles in for an evening of movies starring guns in grand theft auto, wondering in a beer haze; "why can't we just get along". Waking the dead at Arlington National Cemetery with a semi horn, we arrive in DC on the Acadia Ley, to of all places, the Organization of American States.

PATRIARCHY in POLARITY   Deadly Ley Lines   81

Placed at the exact center of the original District of Columbia diamond, the Organization of American States (OAS) is the picture of a Templar commandery, similar to Yale University's 'Skull and Bones Club' also on the Acadia Ley.

Laid out to comply with Masonic Lodge design principles, the backwater swamp location of DC was chosen by George Washington to express Masonic morality and geometric principles as an altruistic empire and new world order at the turning of time.

At the center point of the DC diamond, now made of the district and Arlington County, the OAS is the picture of Ndn magical symbols, whose medallions can be seen beneath its roof overhang. Next door to the Daughters of American Revolution (DAR) the two buildings, OAS and DAR, are divided by C St NW and the Jose Cecilio del Valle Memorial—the exact center of the DC Diamond.

Jose's Memorial comprises a reflecting pool and pavilion. Echoing the god's cry heard from Mexico's human sacrifices, one finds a 20' tall Aztec death mask housed in a pavilion. Centered on the pavilion is a reflecting pool with a statue of Xochipilli, the Aztec god of flowers, sex, drugs, and sports. Xochipilli is called upon in the rite of human sacrifice of those who won the ball game of the day. A picture of the United States, Xochipilli is an Aztec intention set at the center of the DC that could be, through association and history, the god most trusted in deadly America.

With the foundation stone laid by slaves, the United States capital of Washington DC was built upon racism. Its Bill of Rights giving testament to the equal rights of all men are contrary to the facts. Built upon this lie, the U.S. fell short of becoming that "city on the hill" envisioned by the founding Mason fathers. This lie permitted the adversary Ahriman to enter, corrupting its power to serve absolutely. Prospering from a 'Doctrine of Discovery', these Masons took lands and rights from its original peoples who were relegated to POW camps called 'reservations'. Its slave populations, confined to economic ghettos, were empowered by a Black president and military service.

There is a great sin on the soul of America born from its racist past that has yet to be released. At war for all but 20 years of its existence, it is a country with some anger issues—issues perhaps born of racist guilt.

The memory of the Civil War, still being fought between red and blue, was released in ceremony in 2011 to heal the cut of the east to west Missouri Compromise, along the 36.30N line of latitude, that divided the un-United States. Staged in Stone Mountain Georgia, where KKK was instituted, this ceremony of earth-keeper's intention was to release this emotion of the adversary without harm. Answering this call of the earth-keeper, the following day saw a category 5 tornado cut a path of destruction, west to east, across the 42nd parallel of Massachusetts' southern border. Releasing the miasma of empire that prompted the Civil War, the 2011 tornado roared easterward from the 'wip city' of Westfield across the Connecticut River's Civil War Memorial Bridge before removing the roof of the Springfield Armory, who supplied the Union with guns. An empire made of both church and state, the tornado did the same to Cathedral High

School. In a path still visible to satellite, the tornado continued its release of toxic emotion in the land by leveling parts of the city of Munson that made its fortune making Union uniforms and post war granite statuary saluted on yankee town commons. Munson's homes were the picture of Gettysburg Battlefield, with one house scattered to four winds with its neighbors: untouched, full of holes, and twisted off its foundation. Having completed the Earth-Keepers ceremony of release, this tornado returned to its home in the firmament when it crossed the deadly Acadia Ley at Uxbridge, Massachusetts. "Uxbridge Blue' wool was spun into the cloth worn by Union soldiers in both Civil and Indian wars. Given the present state of the union, some work is still needed to heal its trauma triangle.

The Acadia Ley as a line of Western civilization, exhibiting its warring "might is right '' disposition, feeds the Adversary with emotions of fear and hatred, increasing its appetite. With a pyramid mindset and world view ground in Washington Monument's 555' obelisk on the 77tW longitude of English-primed time, the United States serves many masters who are not necessarily by and for its people.

Coursing northeast through the business, Revolutionary and inner city war zones of Baltimore, Philadelphia, Trenton, New Haven and Boston;

this deadly Acadia Ley crosses Cape Ann, the Gulf of Maine ("Remember the Maine"?) to the deadly 60' tidal bores of the Bay of Fund,y and Acadia's Nova Scotia. Leaving Canada's Cape Breton, the ley bisects the arrowhead of Newfoundland pointing the way for the impulse of greco-roman civilization to enter into North America.

A deadly ley of western civilization the Acadia becomes the Arcadia Ley but remains the same ley. Transposing American culture to the east and European culture to the west through the engine of commerce generated by economies of war.

Arcadia Ley

Passing over the North Atlantic Ocean to Ireland its northernmost arc is marked by the Mid-Atlantic Ridge at the edge of the North American Continent. The shortest distance between NYC and London, this jetway  contrails deadly high-altitude pollutants into the troposphere. Also, it was in this same corridor that deadly Nazi submarines sank merchant ships and where the Last Battle of Bismarck occurred during WWII.

Repatriating Ireland's sons from the swamps of New Orleans, anchor is cast on the slave coasts and killing fields of Erin. Parting Atlantic waters, what was Acadia Ley turned into Arcadia Ley; for the ideals of Greek civilization coursing through Arcadia Ley, that makes landfall in Ireland's county Mayo.

Thanks to England's forced diaspora of the Irish, they have flourished the world over. The blossoming Irish population with the introduction of the American potato in 1589 CE, was a problem for the English who coveted their lands. The solution to the 'potato people' came in the spread of a potato blight that resulted in the Irish Famine. A seeming genocide, blight often does occur with mono-crop agriculture. Whatever the cause, British agendas were served in Ireland with the introduction of the blight. John Mitchel in 1861 observed; "The Almighty, indeed, sent the potato blight, but the English created the famine.". This deadly relationship  between the two countries has continued for centuries here and in other polarized countries along the Arcadian Ley.

 When the sun never set on the British Empire their ambitions earn them the deadly ley gold prize. Making fortunes off opium in Asia and the trade triangle of slave, rum, and tobacco in the Atlantic at the expense of others in their exercise of well armed free will, England parlayed industrial might into

wholesale suffering the world over. Their English Empire's sun did set during the world wars, but the trillions remain in the banks of London, Inc..

With wives beheaded, and rebels drawn and quartered, England's deadly history experienced the slaughter of Romans, Saxons, and Vikings creating a collective trauma in their epigenes to validate its bully history.

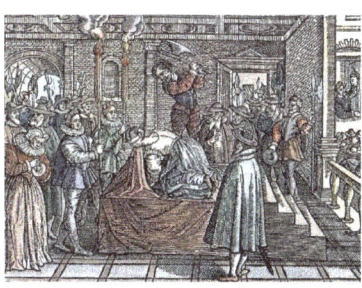

Dublin vs. London, London vs. Brussels (EU), France vs. Germany and so on. The Arcadian Ley hosted the deadly battles that destroyed the Spanish Armada in the Irish Sea; and saw the demise of Napoleon at Waterloo, and Hitler at The Bulge. Presided over by Rome vs. Gaul, and, and, and; this deadly chain of Marley has been carried by lovable humanity for millennia as a habit of those who would be king.

A deadly ley of Western powers, its pathway witnessed the imperial inclinations of the 19th and 20th centuries. Little Belgium saw the genocide of its Jewish population in World Wars, and the brutality of invading German empire's ambitions of the era. Serving out the same brutality in the African Congo of Africa—out of sight out of mind—Belgium's King Leopold II employed the Zappo Zaps tribe of cannibals to do the work of this king against defiant Congolese. Severing of limbs, whippings, rape and all the rest that came along with Leopold's lust for money and blood. Hidden behind the thin facade of civilization and neo-grecco estate walls belies the sacrifice of the 'other', whose bones are its foundation. Contemporarily Belgium is now divided, astride this ley, with talk of session between the bankers in the Flanders and the French speaking farmers of the Wallonia; exemplifying the polarity native to this alignment.

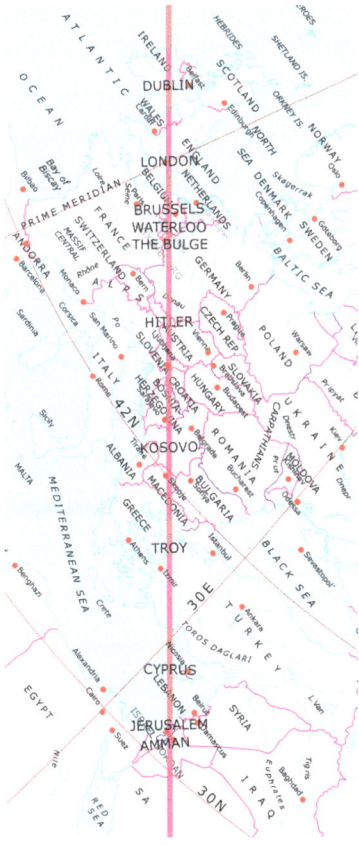

Scaling Austria's Alps, we ski downhill into the maelstrom of Bosnia, Serbia, and Kosovo where this line of war intersects the

42N latitude of the empire. A particularly toxic mix of the modern genocide in the polarity of Christendom and Islam, "Feild of Black Birds', Kosovo, shows the effect of these deadly ley line historicaly.

Navigating the Aegean Sea between Greece and Turkey this deadly Arcadia Ley beaches on the shores of ancient Troy. In the iconic, if not original, Homer saga of 'femme fatale', Helen of Troy was a trophy wife gifted a deadly Trojan Horse. Blowing the nose of Turkey, the ley sails the Mediterranean to divide Cyprus where this battle of Troy continues between Greece and Turkey to this day.

The "rocket's red glare and bombs bursting in air" over the disputed Golan Heights the Party of God (Hezbollah), expresses ley's polarity between Islam and Zion, as the Arcadian Ley enters the Arabian Peninsula. Terminating in the burning sand of Saudi Arabia's 'empty quarter' desert, this deadly ley is overactive at its eastern 19.5 Teotihuacan counterpoint of bordering warring Yemen. Coiled into desert sands the Acadia-Arcadia deadly ley ends in a pool of crude oil that fuels its deadly game.

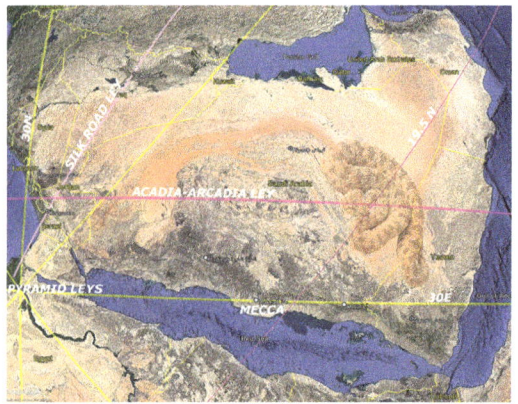

Anchored by the patriarchal cultures of Mexico and Saudi Arabia, the Acadia-Arcadia deadly ley is seen to be brought into balance with the wisdom of the grandmothers. Both Mexico's cartel wars and the Sharia Law of the Saud have resulted in many, many, beheadings in these foundational societies for this world-wide culture of violence. Honor killing in both cultures attesting to the volcanic temperament of the 19.5 latitude, near Mecca, SA. The work of the Adversary, Ahriman, both the drug cartels of Mexico and the oil cartels of Saud exhibit Ahriman's cultivation of Man's lower nature found across this deadly ley line.

Weighing down the spiritual body of the world with its pursuit of Materialism, this yoke, this chain of Marley is bolted to the 19.5 N latitude. This arc of Western powers is rooted in human sacrifice to god and the wills of modern empires. Spanning 150 degrees of longitude, the arc of the Acadia-Arcadia Ley when resolved to a great circle, encompasses Africa, South America, Antarctica, as well as much of Western Europe and Eastern United States in its grip of fear.

Nothing suppresses the spirit of love more than fear. Wrapping the world in fear, this deadly ley is a burden born by this world of sorrows. Freeing the world of this chained yoke of Ahriman frees both land and Man, as "the king (queen) and the land are one". But how is this done?

A ley line of out of control patriarchy, its balance is found in the council of Grandmothers of both the spiritual and material realms. Long excluded, the Grandmothers afford a perspective that benefits seven generations to come, a branch of government appreciated by Native American tribes. December 12, 1531, caught between Aztec blood lust and Spanish Inquisition, the Grandmother of the Universe, Our Lady of Guadalupe, blessed this deadly ley with roses to heal the long suffering souls of the western world. Seeding Earth Merkaba with a love form through the volcanoes of Mexico's hotspot, the miraculous icon awakens the world to its spiritual nature that is the message drawn in the geometry of its image. Appearing to Juan Diego on the slopes of Tepeyac, at the sacred site of Tonantzin, the Aztec mother of the universe, Guadalupe turns human and the world's heart from fear to love through her holy wisdom, bestowed from the spiritual world into deadly ley.

Our Lady of Guadalupe
Geometry Study
by
Peter Champoux
arkhom19@comcast.net
6.20.06

Beijing Ley

Another great circle is the Beijing Ley. This deadly line which parallels the Pacific Ocean's "Ring of Fire" was first discovered during the 2012 Beijing Summer Olympics when it was observed the shortest line between Beijing and Colorado Springs was through the Bering Strait. Drawing out its full circle, this ley was seen to course through natural and cultural features world wide identifying it as a ley line.

Proceeding clockwise from Indonesia through Indochina, China and Russia to the Americas, we begin our journey at the northern end of the island of Sumatra, where Banda Aceh earthquakes tend to generate dramatic and deadly Tsunami waves in the region. While other deadly

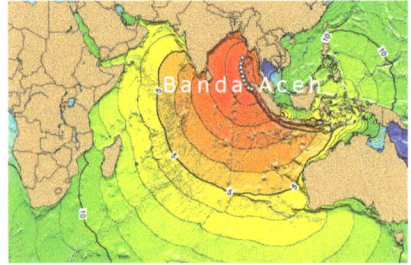

leys were the effect of humans, this ley holds the greatest potential of natural devastation from earthquakes, volcanoes, and floods. That said, there are deadly events aplenty exemplifying Man's inhumanity to Man. Crossing the Andaman Sea, the Malay Peninsula, the golden spires of Bangkok and Indochina come into view from the Gulf of Thailand.

Stopping in for tea with the world's wealthiest monarch King Rama X, the traveler acclimates to the tropics and the noise of Bangkok's deadly traffic. With malaria being a pressing danger of tropical diseases, Thailand's Rama X spends most of his time in Germany avoiding the mosquitoes that took his predecessor Mongkut, King Rama IV. A largely neutral country, it sided with Japan as a lack of choice when invaded as an afterthought to the Pearl Harbor attack on December 8th. Nicknamed the "City of Angels" for its many temples and shrines, Bangkok is believed to be the abode of the gods whose peaceful country is in stark contrast to the rest of these lands between India and China.

Echoing opium poppy production in China, Afghanistan and Mexico, the Golden Triangle of northern Thailand and Laos supplied the deadly world-wide trade of heroin from its mountainous borderlands. Supplying opium laced 'thai sticks' to American servicemen in Vietnam, the Golden Triangle's smoky death followed them home as another PTSD of the war in Vietnam.

Slothing in an opium dream into the war zones

of northern Laos and then North Vietnam, we feel our B-52 rise as its tonnage of bombs are released upon the unsuspecting jungle below. After deploying 7.5 million tons, over thousands of sortes, the 'carpet bombing' of Ho Chi Minh's trail was largely ineffective in stemming the tide of arms and supplies to human waves of N.V.A. regulars and Viet Cong fighters against French and American invaders.

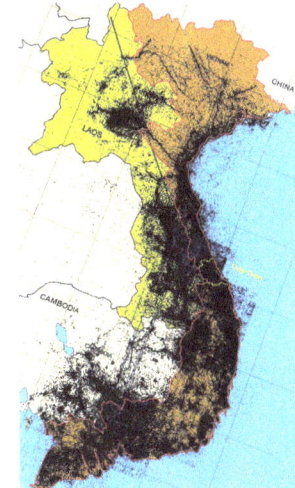

In the secret war of 1963, the USAF dropped 250 million anti-personnel cluster bombs on the Laotian stretch of the Beijing Ley, 80 million of which remain as deadly unexploded ordnance across the northern central plain of Laos. Known as the Plain of Jars, this megalithic archaeological landscape is an ancient neck of the woods littered not only with bombs, but also with megalithic Jars used for burials between 1240 to 660 BC. The jars vary in height and diameter between three and six feet and are all hewn from monolithic rock. Their shape is cylindrical with the bottom always wider than the top. It is of curious how the cluster bombs are a fractal shape of these funerary jars in a metaphorical way, attacking not only the living but the ancestors as well. The 90 Jar sites, each with up to 400 jars, are scattered like the cluster bombs over this Laotian central plain of the Xiangkhoang Plateau, making this one of the world's most dangerous graveyards.

In 1995, Vietnam released its official estimate of those killed during the Vietnam War to be as many as 2,000,000 civilians on both sides and some 1,100,000 North Vietnamese and Viet Cong fighters. The U.S. military has estimated that between 200,000 and 250,000 South Vietnamese soldiers died. This along with the well tabulated 58,220 deaths of Americans in the waste of this conflict. The number of vaporized trees, rice plants and other flora and fauna of its jungles remains uncounted.

Crossing into mainland China, on the supply roads of the Vietnam wars, we stop at the cross road of the Silk Road Ley for further tabulations of what was a really tough 20th Century for the Chinese peoples.

Orchestrated by the powers of Beijing there has been:

105,000 Victims: Dynastic and Republican China

632,000 Victims: Warlord China

2,724,000 Victims: The Nationalist Period

10,216,000 Victims: The Sino-Japanese War

3,949,000 Victims: Japanese Mass Murder in China

4,968,000 Victims: The Civil War

8,427,000 Victims: The People's Republic of China,Totalization Period

7,474,000 Victims: Collectivization and "The Great Leap Forward"

10,729,000 Victims: The Great Famine and Retrenchment Period

7,731,000 Victims: The "Cultural Revolution"

874,000 Victims: Liberalization,

for a grand total 57 million 829 Thousand deaths in not that many years.

Antithetical to China's traditional values of harmony, benevolence, righteousness, courtesy, wisdom, honesty, loyalty, and filial piety, PRC has short circuited its chinese made motherboard. Oh... the trauma of it all! "Qing zài duō dian yāpiàn."

On line to Beijing, the next stop on this orient express is White Emperor City. A place of poets who defined Chinese character values, Baidicheng in Chinese, the White Emperor City was once shrouded in the mists of the Yangtze River narrows. Now a still backwater of the Three Gorges Dam, at the iconic mountainous Kuimen Gates, Baidicheng is now an island memory of China's creative past. At the pinch point of converging mountainand river fingers,..aka dragon and tiger, WEC is the center of southern China scribed as center to south coast arc.

Once a deadly water, the Yangtze River has been temporarily tamed by its Three Gorges Dam impoundment. Now tamed, the Yangtze chi dampened, a 'damp' inflamed constitution would be a diagnosis in Chinese medicine.

A constitutional weakness of the immune system, Covid-19 germinated in nearby Wuhan... resulting in 15 million deaths worldwide. A deadly ley line indeed.

Feng shui of China suggests the PRC, like the Yangtze, has blocked chi, chi-na man!

Standing down tanks we enter Tiananmen Squar,e bowing three times to Great Khan Xi for a visa through Meridian Gate to Beijing's 'Forbidden City'. To think, once beheaded for entrance, we now stroll its 9,999 rooms, yet heads still roll down the emperor's staircase.

On a personal note, when attending a Catholic elementary school during the Cold War students were fed violently descriptive comic books on the Chinese communist's treatment of priests in China. An anti-communist terror campaign on the part of Cardinal Spellman (spell is right!), nuns had a child sized box at the ready, post marked Beijing, China, where misbehaving children were to be sent. Thankfully only once was a kid heard screaming in repentance as they were dragged box and all down the hallway to the awaiting imagined postman. A well founded terror.

Goose stepping into Manchuria of Northeast China, to droning Erhu, we cross its Japanese killing fields into the gulags of far eastern Russia.

In a heading towards the Bering Strait, the Beijing Ley is focused by the metallic minerals of the gulag Kolyma. A frozen land, it is said a million perished in transport, or by labored starvation, in the gulags of subarctic Kolyma. Populated by Stalin's enemies, real and imagined, Russia's brain trust disappeared; as it is unknown how many died, as all traces of their existence was purged from public record and DNA.

In the book 'The Gulag Archipelago', Aleksandr Solizhenitsyn characterizes Kolyma as the "pole of cold and cruelty" in Stalin's gulag based penal system. It begs the question: how many Solzhenitsyn, and other such creative's contributions got lost in the shuffle, depriving seventh generations to come?

Escaping the gulag, we cross the Bering Strait from Russia's Big Diomede Island to Alaska's Little Diomede across the time-killing 'International Date Line'...from yesterday to tomorrow. Two and a half miles distant between the Diomedes, one can see the 'other' across 20 hours of lost time as witness to eternal present.

At its northernmost apex, the Beijing Ley crosses the Bering Land Bridge and Yukon

River, brushing the Arctic Circle before turning southwest through America's western ranges. By Denali Peak, over scattering caribou, the Beijing Ley enters into Alaska's Bermuda Triangle. Known for its 20,000 unexplained disappearances, the Alaska Triangle is home to the deadly High-frequency Active Auroral Research Program (HAARP). Described both in conspiracy and inventor's patent, HAARP weaponises the Ionosphere bringing death through: tsunami, hurricane, and targeting weather and electromagnetics. As with any antenna system, the channel can be changed.

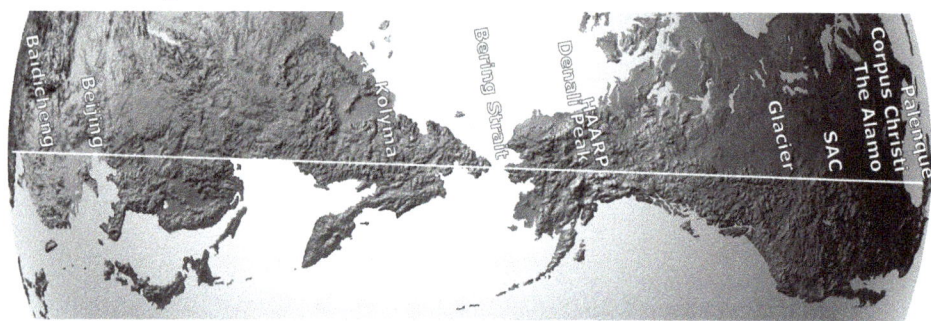

Continuing Beijing's straight track through Sasquatch country, we run for it southeast between the Rocky Mountain and Coastal ranges, to the U.S. border and Glacier National Park.

Called, "Backbone of the World" by local Blackfoot Indians, Glacier and nearby vortex of Kalispell are more megaforms that tune the Beijing Ley, deadly or lively.

Both lively and deadly, the Yellowstone supervolcano is so super it can do both on this ley. A fountain of gasses, geysers and grizzlies today... civilization ending volcanic winter tomorrow, as serendipity and caldera permit. Yellowstone's rumbling Rhode Island size magma dome, if released, would kill 100,000 in its blast, with many more to stumble over the pests that follow. Leaning towards the wild, Yellowstone growls

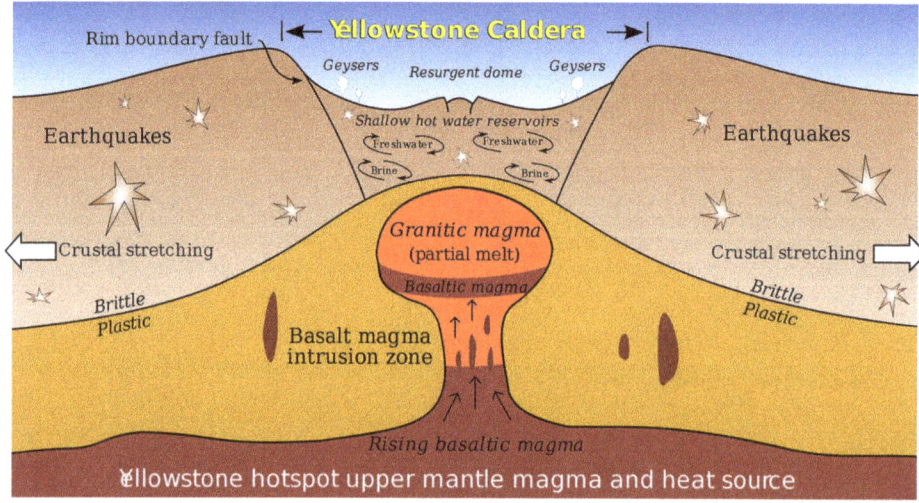

like a Sasquatch from the forest's edge and might just throw some stones.

When touched, rock becomes stone and culture. Anthroposophia has it that gnomes of knowledge are released when rock is split and emotions are released by hurricanes. Examining Earth for first cut, a stone mason would hammer the Beijing Ley as the plane of least resistance to split this world in two. Each 57 million deaths, and 250 million cluster bombs, and HAARP, and, and, and… are hammer blows along this path of least resistance as "cleft for thee". It is the case with granite that each hammer blow increases its piezoelectric charge. Applied in scale as earthquakes along these deadly tectonic planes, one can imagine that this is how the earth renews its magnetic field every 25,000 +- years.

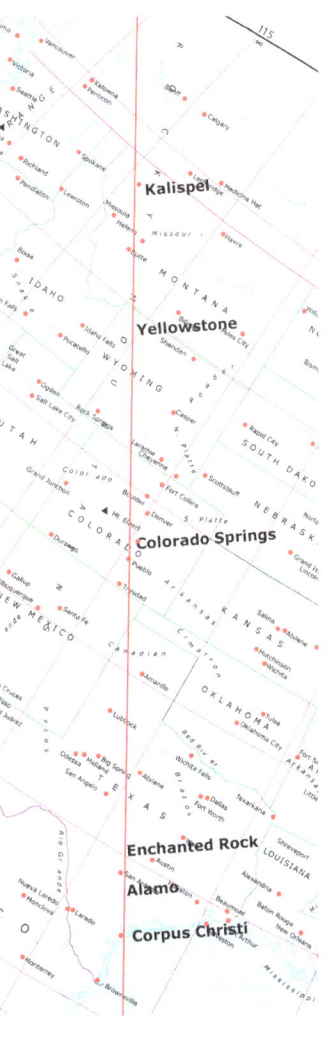

Aligned with the Wind River Range, Crow and Shoshone nations, the Beijing Ley tracks near the South Pass of the Oregon Trail, the trail that replaced Native Americans and their way of life with Colonial Americans. In a pioneering spirit of empire, backed up with a 'doctrine of discovery, we enter Colorado via horseshoe shaped North Park, where China's ley crests Berthoud Pass, crossing the 'front range' of the Rocky Mountains. From Pikes Peak; Colorado Springs, the USAF Academy and Cheyenne Mountain' USAF Strategic Air Command (SAC) can all be seen. Another node of fear and death, SAC, deep in the mountain, is the world's most deadly node, with its trigger finger on civilization ending nuclear missles.

Ugg…Fear, the only emotion common to all. Love…not so much, with love as unique as a face and character. The go to emotion for crowd control, FEAR transmits quickly through HAARP tuned ionosphere and ley tuned geosphere; the same goes for love.. Aligned with SAC and HAARP, the Beijing Ley comes into focus as a macroscape linking eastern and western hemispheres through north and south polar circles. The Beijing Ley's encircles the Pacific Ocean as a fire of fear to be tempered in ocean water, 'turning swords into plowshares' sometime between yesterday and tomorrow.

Escaping the reverie of Peak's view, our imagination looks southeast across Texas plain, to Enchanted Rock and The Alamo, to gulf's edge with Corpus Christi.

The center of the Texas Earth Ring, Enchanted Rock is a ley marker of granite in a sea of Texas limestone along the Beijing Ley. Deemed spooky and sacred to local Tonkawa, Apache and Comanche 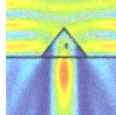 tribes, Enchanted Rock's piezoelectric granite embedded in dielectric limestone, generates a field much like that of the Great Pyramid, whose deadly ley also crosses Enchanted Rock. Ley lines and their nodes are neutral with polarity directed and attracted by the emotions entrained by activities on the ley line. Fear in, fear out. Love in, love out.

Remembering the Alamo in Texas, along the Beijing deadly ley, is a story of fortune's reversal. Instigated by illegal immigration into Mexico, whose use of slaves was also illegal, the government of Mexico was forced to act in defense of its sovereign lands and laws. Santa Anna's attack on the Alamo was permitted as the defenders of the Alamo were considered pirates, circumventing existing treaties with the United States. As pirates, all were to be executed by the army of Mexico.

Both a sacred site, as consecrated mission church, and as a battlefield; the convention of sanctuary was desecrated. Alamo, translated from Spanish as Poplar, the trees white leaves are associated with old age. Sacred to ancient Greeks, the Poplar was said to grow at the entrance to Hades, the underworld, the "Realm of the Dead".

An iconic event in American and Texas history, the Alamo and its 'last stand' was made in defense of liberty in the American imagination. The Alamo, more than any battle, instilled the fortress mentality in the American character. Given the current state of the Texas border with illegal immigration and the drug cartel enslaved arriving as barbarians at the gate, the shoe is on the other foot that treads this deadly ley. With eucharistic benediction "the body of Christ" is proclaimed by Alamo's Franciscan priest. Both dead and living, the body of Christ is like the memory of the Alamo, both living and dead in the American heart.

Corpus Christi Texas, our next node on the Beijing Ley, was so named by Spaniard captain Alonso de Pineda when its green bay was first seen by this European on the Feast Day of Corpus Christi in 1519.

Its large, shallow bay makes Corpus Christi an ideal feeding place for birds. The "Bird Capital" of North America, Corpus Christi as "America's birdiest place" is located on an avian ley line between North and South America that both humans and birds follow during seasonal migrations. Battered by Gulf of Mexico hurricanes and battled over by Union and Confederate forces, Corpus Christi is seen with a dove of hope hovering above after storm and blood sacrifice.

Leaving the United States the Beijing Ley crosses the gulf waters to the Yucatan and archeological site of Palenque, Mexico. The cultural center of an enlightened ruler Pacal Voltan, the treasures of this place included the well known "astronaut" sarcophagus lid found beneath the Temple of Inscriptions. Abandoned by 800CE, this Mayan city state's population disappeared into the jungles at the same time as other Mayan city states of the region when the Mayan civilization collapsed  under the deathly stress of prolonged drought. Leaving a record in stone as memory of their passing, the Maya of Mexico live on without need of city or state.

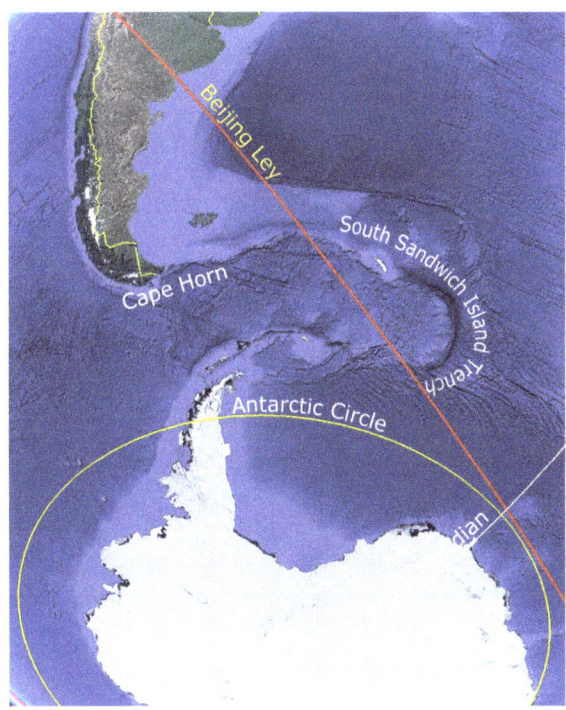

Aligned along the serpentine 'Ring of Fire' around the Pacific Ocean, our deadly ley crosses the volcanoes of Guatemala hugging the straight coast of Peru along the Peru-Chile Trench. Passing the once great Inca civilizations, now a memory and ruin, the "disappeared" of Chile's Junta are remembered too. As they are remebered, the Beijing Ley descends the Andes Mountains into Argentina and the extreme depths of the South Sandwich Trench squeezed between the tails of South America and Antarctica. Rounding the ice fields of the South Pole's Antarctic Circle, at ley's southern most point of time's Prime Meridian, we ride the telluric current of Earth's electromagnetic field northward through the Indian Ocean, completing our great circle back to the equatorial heat of Sumatra.

From polar and time's extremes, the Beijing Ley rounds both Bering Strait and Cape Horn from north to south and back again in a deadly historic dance between yesterday and tomorrow. In the timeless etheric body of Christ his blood stains earth red as Colorado. Riding the waves of electromagnetic light through a ring of life, HAARP tuned ionosphere messages the Earth of the atom's demise and its rebirth as a holy water bonding of mutual suffering and mutual peace; rejecting Mutual Assured Destruction (MAD) as policy.

Crossing Waves

Enchained with deadly ley lines, the living Earth is choked with their tightening grip. Losing their grip is what we explore next, examining the crossing points along their course. Rivers, winds, underground streams, mountains ranges, were ever they cross result in a vortex of counter opposing streams. A modern awareness of Sedona, Arizona's vortex are by example the result of multiple ley lines and 'Earth Rings' crossings as waves caught up in its paraamagnetic rock formations whose shape mimic the vortex that permeate this little big city.

Not discussed much in our treaties, 'Earth Rings', one might say, are a circular ley lines. Sedona is in a place on Earth's consciousness membrane where these rings interpenetrate each other. In total the Earth is seen as a cell, Earth-Cell. A cell functions, according to the biologist Bruce Lipton, is governed by its membrane exchanging information from inside and from outside to maintain stathis of the biology it supports. What serves the cell in the regulatory exchange of this information are geometric and centric Integral Membrane Proteins (IMPs). In the fractal composition of the universe, 'Earth Rings' serve this capacity for Earth-Cell.

Any line projected around a sphere forms a great circle or equatorial circumference. With the Earth shaped more elliptical than circular, things get messy with spherical projects made possible with Google Earth whose software is used here and in other ley studies. Perhaps in the near future, a more accurate model will be available to more accurately map great circle leys. With the exception of the latitude rings mentioned, all of these deadly leys are world encompassing 'Earth Rings'. Coursing through world wide Earth-Cell IMPs (Integral Membrane Plutons) these deadly lines message its bio with discordance that result in living Earth's response to these emotions of war with inflammation to purge itself. An example of this being the Herat, Afghanistan earthquake on the Silk Road Ley that followed the Hamas attack of early December 2023 in Gaza on the same ley. With Gaza being in the Great Pyramid Earth Ring and Herat in the Iranistan Earth Ring, the Silk Road Ley signaled Earthquake as release of an emotion it could no longer bear after all the successive conflicts along the Silk Road Ley from river to sea.

Where vortexes occur, objects tend to spin endlessly until pulled into its depths. Similarly where streams of emotion carried upon deadly ley lines converge, those emotions tend to get stuck until pulled under and transformed into another form of energy. It is at these crossing of leys where emotions of war get stuck until released by an emotion of a different color.

Observing history along these lines, we see the history of war repeating itself, often with antecedents for wars past. A neutral field until entrained with frequency, leys lines tend to attract whatever has been programmed by its history in total, attracting the same.

With its conditioning laid bare, it is hoped the Earth consciousness membrane field that is humanity can shift their frequencies from fear and hatred to love and empathy. A tall order for a humanity so conditioned by the Adversary and the disconnecting effects of free will to come together as a common will to heal this world illness. Counteracting the Adversary's agenda to suppress the elevation of homo spiritus into its full expression, deadly ley lines are an opportunity for humanity to exercise its contrary impulse, reprogramming ley and planet with that 'woke' love and empathy. The place to start this remedial action are at the crossing waves of these deadly leys.

Great Pyramid

Perhaps the most glaring vortex at crossing leys is the Great Pyramid. A heresy in 'New Age' circles, the Great Pyramid as vortex of fear and death is contrary to the messaging of the many who guide pilgrimages there. A model of top-down economic, social order, nutritional, and pyramidal schemes; the Pyramid has been misread to royalties advantage messaging this meme into world consciousness at the center of its membrane's landmass. Counteracting this empire's genocidal force over the world a simple adjustment is required.

The most loving, empathic and spiritually nurturing force in the world and solar systems are the celestial waters Creation. Not often, if not ever, noted in treaties on the Great Pyramid is that its apex angle is the same angle as water's bonding angle of its two hydrogen to oxygen to form the molecule of water. Connecting biosphere to hydrogen as solar logos, celestial and terrestrial waters informed earth-cell with stathis with its perfection of form when first built. Degenerated into a ruin by its misappropriation, the Pyramid serves water's opposite seen in the earth rings and deadly ley lines vortexing at this crossing of waves.

The Pyramid's shift back to its orginal geometry water is offered as an alternative to present pagan symbol and mausoleum. A life affirming form as water is associated with the Holy Spirit (or Hagia Sophia), see the pyramid as a blessing of holy water's blessings. In fact, witnessing the flow of cleansing scared waters flowing through the crossing deadly leys of the Pyramids purifies and ameliorates blood's emotions of fear held in the earth of these death repeating lines.

Boston, Massachusetts

Another prominent crossing of deadly ley lines vortex in Boston, Massachusetts, USA. On the empire wave of the 42nd latitude at the intersection of the First Nations and Acadia leys, Boston coaleases as a landform into nested hexagons. A gematria of harmony, its interpenetrating triangles speak to a balance—as above so below. Its thigh geometric locking into these crossing waves. A mini IMPs very near the geologic center of circular North Americ,a its influence is far reaching.

It was from Boston that the first salvoes of the Indian Wars were shot. And it was through Boston the last of these wars were healed in the return of Wounded Knee artifacts to the Lakota of South Dakota, where those wars ended. Called the Boston States by Nova Scotians of the Acadia Ley, it is through the coherent waters of Boston Harbor this ley is cleared of trauma's memory with infinite's wave. At a nexus of regional and continental leys, ley healing transmitted into, above and around Boston would ride on the Masonic Lodge tuned civic landscape from capitol dome to golden capital dome.

Three Borders

An obscure but strategically important corner of the world, the three border zone along the Tumen River bordering China, North Korea and Russia is the center point of another Earth Ring scribed by the arc of Japan's island chain. The only rail line linking Russia to North Korea, this bridge over the river Tumen has conveyed weaponry to and fro for a century.

An atomic earth ring, whose circumference marks Beijing, witnessed the destruction of Hiroshima, Nagasaki, Fukushima and the nuclear proliferation of the Korean Peninsula. A powderkeg, the tension between these adjoining political denominations dominate its horizons.

At the crossing waves of the 42nd's propensity towards empire and the Pyramid's north east deadly ley, a triple vortex of communist trauma is spun.

Opposing a sovereign soul's impulse towards freedom, under the miasma of empire, Japan crossed its sea into the lands of the Mongols in a tsunami of death at the onset of WWII. Still fresh in the collective memory of the region, its trauma triangle still seeks the hero.

A convergence point of river, international borders and ley lines, this point of war calls for its balance. United as nations by common Tumen waters, and all members of the United Nations, the United Nations prayer for peace is called for. Spoken as a balanced vortex and visualized as a geometry of gravity, this prayer's intention transforms the feared vortex of a nuclear death to a grail cup of life. Inclusive of the entire Earth Ring, the tensions of peninsula and islands are seen in conjoint creation with joy for all in its contemplation.

Fertile Crescent

Centered on the border swamps, where war dead were piled as roadbeds in the Iraq/Iran war, the crossing waves of the Fertile Crescent is where modern civilization began in ancient Sumeria. Criss-crossed by deadly leys, the Earth Ring is marked by the radius of the Euphrates River from swamp delta to source in Armenia.

Hoop Rolling the Euphrates Earth Ring the 42nd ley of empire keeps its deadly spin in motion as a game of humanity's youth. Its hoop clad in religions had spokes drawn by the meanderings of Abraham. Home ground of Cain and Abel, Sunni and Shia, Adam and Eve, Jesus and Mary and the hanging garden of Babylon; it was from this place the clay tablets of Hamaribi were plagiarized as foundation for Abrahamic religions. As a spoke in its hoop that spoke a curse against the "one true god, above all others", cycles of religious supremacy have plagued these lands where the Silk Road and Arcadian leys cross waves.

A native impulse "towards to one truth the covers" has been declared by each religion growing from the Cresent. This spiritual adventure that is the consicious human has been quested since Neandrathals first ingested psychotropic sacraments seeking answer to the Great Mystery. In incremental evolutions of religious thought, humanity has come ever closer to that truth with every iteration. At campfires along the trade routes through the Crescent, where all the world religions gathered, they learned each of their religion's response was to the same divine impulse, and sufism was born. Sufism, propagating a sovereign relationship with all that is a collective yet individualized stream of consciousness lifts the whole world towards this one source and one force; or as the Lakota ndns would say, "Mitakuye Oyasin", all my relations. Addressing this same sovereign source and force within Jesus exemplified Christ in the etheric and bid us to seek the Christ within. A dangerous notion to those who would control its impulse through state sponsored religions who gave no quarter to such heresy.

Rogue Waves

Portala, Lhasa Tibet, the city of heaven at the crossing of Great Pyramid latitude and Silk Road deadly leys ignored suffering like a starving Buddha until a Chinese invasion taught true suffering to the monks who brought their way of being to the west in diaspora.

Kosovo, field of black birds at the crossing of the 42nd and Arcadian waves of war rolling over it from north, south, east, and west act out the their entrained thought forms without reason as release valve for the Balkans.

Like surfers caught in the undertow of crossing waves humanity have rode their curled and suffocated under their weight in wipe-out. Rinse and repeat until mastered the exercise of free will has its challenges but its diamond sutra will hopefully, eventually, shine for the benefit of All That Is.

Answering the Call

This short listing of the crossing waves illustrates the blending of cultural dysfunction in place. The frequency of every ley is the aggregate of events along its path. Crossing waves present the greatest opportunity to transform its frequency into a higher state of being. Methods to accomplish this are many, with more solutions, inspired by revelation, delivered daily in these times of spiritual transformation.

Holy Grail Vortex, Infinity Waves, Prayer Wheels, Treasure Vases, and co-creations of the like, are all effective when changing the frequency of the mass.

Simply, the admonishment to "Think, Holy Water", as a unifying field, may be all that is necessary to shift humanity's consciousness and that of the world.

CONCLUSION

Whether or not this little big-book, with its lack of scholarship, has convinced you the reader of the existence of invisible lines is immaterial. It is sprititual in nature. In the realm of belief, or lack thereof, ley lines are seen by their effects. Deadly Ley Lines are seen, known and experienced in the levels of fear and death lived along their pathways. Belief is a popular emotion and is often sited in our social lives in context to politics, religion, and food choices. Whether one convinces the other of the efficacy of this belief is also a spiritualization of matter. Writing and reading about man's inhumanity, throughout recorded history has been disheartening but 'belief' remains in the innate goodness of humanity.

We have all participated, to some degree, to the suffering on earth as an unavoidable consequence of being born. In the free egoic exercise of free will in this lifetime, or others as reincarnates, we have found ourselves at one apex or another to that 'trauma triangle', acting out as: pertitrator, victim, or hero. The simplest of necessities required to provide for a household places one within this triangle of trauma within Earth's economy of profit through suffering. Played out in scale from emperor, to nation, to candlestick maker, someone profits from another's loss. "That's the way life is!" Or is it?

In this exploration of the world we have attempted to illustrate how deadly economies of scale have coalesced into focused streams of consciousness that tends towards repetition. Showing the Earth as enchained, like the 'Ghost of Christmas Past', we can learn from the errors of 'Marley' and hold hope for a new beginning free of the chains of materialism.

Deadly ley lines, we might conclude, is the spiritual world quite literally bleeding through into the material world. Being invisible not unlike the bearded one source-one force. In the lectures of Anthroposophist, Rudolf Steiner, it is posited that ever increasing violent world wars on Earth are from the frustration of materialist souls who find themselves in the spiritual realms without the spiritual skills to enjoy its blissful state of being. A setup by Ahriman, the adversary, denial of the spiritual nature inherent to a sovereign soul of humanity seeks to deprive Creation of its gifts in its relentless quest to destroy humanity's garden.

Cinched ever tighter by fear and ego's dominion, the chains of materialism expressed as deadly lines, in conscious awareness, are a clarion call to return to fear's opposite, love. Up to anthropomorphised Earth-Cell to free itself from Ahriman's chains, the cell membrane consciousness of life is freed when brought to the light of awareness. No longer can the wizard behind tatared curtain be ignored with excuses of, 'its human nature'. Darkness exists only in fear, in the absence of that which is real, Light.

Given a bad rap by the powers that be, seeking control as emperor and priests, the gift of love to the world that was the Christ is the only force and source capable of transfiguring these chains of fears to the warmth of love. May the great mystery that is life never be solved. However, the mystery of Golgotha, that is Christ renewal in love is a force gifted the etheric body of the world and held at bay by the ley chains of war. Transfiguring the world as he did on Golgotha, Christ waters flow as love via Jerusalem's etheric ley lines warming and dissolving these chains that bind time to fear. The simple act of bearing witness to Christ's warmth bonding with the water geometry of the Great Pyramid's ley lines seats that presence in place transforming the pyramid's dissonance. Feeling this warmth flowing from ones own heart through Acadia and Arcadia leys, around the world on the 42nd latitude of empire, and the Beijing Ley permeates the world membrane consciousness with this warmth of love.

It can not be emphasized enough the power of intent (prayer) in resonant alignment with the One Source and One Force that is Love. Through this love permeating Earth's etheric body expressed as ley lines it rains in the desert and fills the lakes of California in one season; and turns Earth's economy of suffering into one of giving, in coherent resonance with Christ in the etheric.

Ley lines cohere along strategic alignments that unites humanity as empire, or economy, or force for good. The crossing waves of these leys are interface portals where love's programming are entered into the planetary mainframe. Such was the programming of Golgotha that has taken these centuries to rewrite, reboot, and transfigure.

With the advent of the world wide web, the web of life and death has been made intimate, experienced in the moment numbing or awakening empathy to suffering. With geographic modeling tools and the view from space of our blue-green Earth, adversarial us and them become distant to a relationship with, 'All That Is'.

Curbed by a guided collective belief the sovereign soul acting in free will has been frowned upon by collective belief that has suppressed the indigenous mind expressed as heretic and 1st Nation Peoples. While a belief held by a group in common support agreed upon worldview it limits the miraculous abilities of the sovereign soul to transform the world in healing, loving partnership so needed to overcome the material adversary to the spiritual world.

Nothing happens in the material world without first being visioned in the spiritual world. As physical, etheric, astral, and spiritual beings Humanities place is to serve as witness in the physical for a spiritual impulse. The Christ impulse for instance.

A common unity of souls on both sides of the Threshold, elemental and angelic, we serve together to restore 'The Garden' as sovereign spiritual beings having a physical experience along Earth's Deadly Ley Lines.

www.ingramcontent.com/pod-product-compliance
Lightning Source LLC
Chambersburg PA
CBHW062102290426
44110CB00022B/2688